THIS
CRAFT OF
VERSE

The
Charles Eliot
Norton Lectures
1967–1968

THIS CRAFT OF VERSE

JORGE LUIS BORGES

Edited by Calin-Andrei Mihailescu

HARVARD UNIVERSITY PRESS □ 2000

Cambridge, Massachusetts, and London, England

Frontispiece: Borges lecturing at Harvard University, 1967. Photo by
Christopher S. Johnson; courtesy of *Harvard Magazine.*

Library of Congress Cataloging-in-Publication Data
Borges, Jorge Luis, 1899–1986
This craft of verse / Jorge Luis Borges;
edited by Calin-Andrei Mihailescu.
p. cm.—(The Charles Eliot Norton lectures; 1967–1968)
ISBN 0-674-00290-3 (alk. paper)
I. Poetry—History and criticism. I. Mihailescu, Calin-Andrei, 1956–
II. Title. III. Series.
PN1064.B67 2000
809.1—dc21
00-033541

CONTENTS

1 The Riddle of Poetry *1*

2 The Metaphor *21*

3 The Telling of the Tale *43*

4 Word-Music and Translation *57*

5 Thought and Poetry *77*

6 A Poet's Creed *97*

Notes *125*

"Of This and That Versatile Craft"
by Calin-Andrei Mihailescu 143

Index *151*

At the outset, I would like to give you fair warning of what to expect—or rather, of what not to expect—from me. I find that I have made a slip in the very title of my first lecture. The title is, if we are not mistaken, "The Riddle of Poetry," and the stress of course is on the first word, "riddle." So you may think the riddle is all-important. Or, what might be still worse, you may think I have deluded myself into believing that I have somehow discovered the true reading of the riddle. The truth is that I have no revelations to offer. I have spent my life reading, analyzing, writing (or trying my hand at writing), and enjoying. I found the last to be the most important thing of all. "Drinking in" poetry, I have come to a final conclusion about it. Indeed, every time I am faced with a blank page, I feel that I have to rediscover literature for myself. But the past is of no avail whatever to me. So, as I have said, I have only my perplexities to offer you. I am nearing seventy. I have given the major part of my life to literature, and I can offer you only doubts.

The great English writer and dreamer Thomas De Quincey wrote—in some of the thousands of pages of his fourteen volumes—that to discover a new problem was quite as important as discovering the solution to an old one. But I cannot even offer you that; I can offer you only time-honored perplexities. And yet, why need I worry about this? What is a history of philosophy, but a history of the perplexities of the Hindus, of the Chinese, of the Greeks, of the Schoolmen, of Bishop Berkeley, of Hume, of Schopenhauer, and so on? I merely wish to share those perplexities with you.

Whenever I have dipped into books of aesthetics, I have had an uncomfortable feeling that I was reading the works of astronomers who never looked at the stars. I mean that they were writing about poetry as if poetry were a task, and not what it really is: a passion and a joy. For example, I have read with great respect Benedetto Croce's book on aesthetics, and I have been handed the definition that poetry and language are an "expression." Now, if we think of an expression of something, then we land back at the old problem of form and matter; and if we think about the expression of nothing in particular, that gives us really nothing. So we respectfully receive that definition, and then we go on to something else. We go on to poetry; we go on to life. And life is, I am sure, made of poetry. Poetry is not alien—poetry is, as we shall see, lurking round the corner. It may spring on us at any moment.

Now, we are apt to fall into a common confusion. We think, for example, that if we study Homer, or the *Divine Comedy,* or Fray Luis de León, or *Macbeth,* we are studying poetry. But books are only occasions for poetry.

I think Emerson wrote somewhere that a library is a kind of magic cavern which is full of dead men. And those dead men can be reborn, can be brought to life when you open their pages.

Speaking about Bishop Berkeley (who, may I remind you, was a prophet of the greatness of America), I remember he wrote that the taste of the apple is neither in the apple itself—the apple cannot taste itself—nor in the mouth of the eater. It requires a contact between them. The same thing happens to a book or to a collection of books, to a library. For what is a book in itself? A book is a physical object in a world of physical objects. It is a set of dead symbols. And then the right reader comes along, and the words—or rather the poetry behind the words, for the words themselves are mere symbols—spring to life, and we have a resurrection of the word.

I am reminded now of a poem you all know by heart; but you will never have noticed, perhaps, how strange it is. For perfect things in poetry do not seem strange; they seem inevitable. And so we hardly thank the writer for his pains. I am thinking of a sonnet written more than a hundred years ago by a young man in London (in Hampstead, I think), a young man who died of lung disease, John Keats, and of his famous and perhaps hackneyed sonnet "On First Looking into Chapman's Homer." What is strange about that poem—and I thought of this only three or four days ago, when I was pondering this lecture—is the fact that it is a poem written about the poetic experience itself. You know it by heart, yet I would like you to hear once more the surge and thunder of its final lines,

> Then felt I like some watcher of the skies
> When a new planet swims into his ken;
> Or like stout Cortez when with eagle eyes

He stared at the Pacific—and all his men
look'd at each other with a wild surmise—
Silent, upon a peak in Darien.

Here we have the poetic experience itself. We have George Chapman, the friend and rival of Shakespeare, being dead and suddenly coming to life when John Keats read his *Iliad* or his *Odyssey*. I think it was of George Chapman (but I cannot be sure, as I am not a Shakespearean scholar) that Shakespeare was thinking when he wrote: "Was it the proud full sail of his great verse, / Bound for the prize of all too precious you?"[1]

There is a word that seems to me very important: "On *First* Looking into Chapman's Homer." This "first" may, I think, prove most helpful to us. At the very moment I was going over those mighty lines of Keats's, I was thinking that perhaps I was only being loyal to my memory. Perhaps the real thrill I got out of the verses by Keats lay in that distant moment of my childhood in Buenos Aires when I first heard my father reading them aloud. And when the fact that poetry, language, was not only a medium for communication but could also be a passion and a joy—when this was revealed to me, I do not think I understood the words, but I felt that something was happening to me. It was happening not to my mere intelligence but to my whole being, to my flesh and blood.

Going back to the words "On *First* Looking into Chapman's Homer," I wonder if John Keats felt that thrill after he had gone through the many books of the *Iliad* and the *Odyssey*. I think the *first* reading of a poem is a true one, and after that we delude ourselves into the belief that the sensation, the impression, is repeated. But, as I say, it may be mere loyalty, a mere trick of the memory, a mere confusion between our passion and the passion we once felt. Thus, it might be said that poetry is a new experience every time. Every time I read a poem, the experience happens to occur. And that is poetry.

I read once that the American painter Whistler was in a café in Paris, and people were discussing the way in which heredity, the environment, the political state of the times, and so on influence the artist. And then Whistler said, "Art happens." That is to say, there is something mysterious about art. I would like to take his words in a new sense. I shall say: *Art happens every time we read a poem.* Now, this may seem to clear away the time-honored notion of the classics, the idea of everlasting books, of books where one may always find beauty. But I hope I am mistaken here.

Perhaps I may give a brief survey of the history of books. So far as I can remember, the Greeks had no great use for books. It is a fact, indeed, that most of the great teachers of mankind have been not writers but speakers. Think of Pythagoras, Christ, Socrates, the Buddha, and so on. And since I have spoken of Socrates, I would like to say something about Plato. I remember Bernard Shaw said that Plato was the dramatist who invented Socrates, even as the four evangelists were the dramatists who invented Jesus. This may be going too far, but there is a certain truth in it. In one of the dialogues of Plato, he speaks about books in a rather disparaging way: "What is a book? A book seems, like a picture, to be a living being; and yet if we ask it something, it does not answer. Then we see that it is dead."[2] In order to make the book into a living thing, he invented—happily for us—the Platonic dialogue, which forestalls the reader's doubts and questions.

But we might say also that Plato was wistful about Socrates. After Socrates' death, he would say to himself, "Now, what would Socrates have said about this particular doubt of mine?" And then, in order to hear once again the voice of the master he loved, he wrote the dialogues. In some of these dialogues, Socrates stands for the truth. In others, Plato has dramatized his many moods. And some of those dialogues come to no conclusion whatever, because Plato was thinking as he wrote them; he did not know the last page when he wrote the first. He was letting his mind wander, and he was dramatizing that mind into many people. I suppose his chief aim was the illusion that, despite the fact that Socrates had drunk the hemlock, Socrates was still with him. I feel this to be true because I have had many masters in my life. I am proud to be a disciple—a good disciple, I hope. And when I think of my father, when I think of the great Jewish-Spanish author Rafael Cansinos-Asséns,[3] when I think of Macedonio Fernández,[4] I would also like to hear their voices. And sometimes I train my voice into a trick of imitating their voices, in order that I may think as they would have thought. They are always around me.

There is another sentence, in one of the Fathers of the Church. He said that it was as dangerous to put a book into the hands of an ignorant man as to put a sword into the hands of children. So books, to the ancients, were mere makeshifts. In one of his many letters, Seneca wrote against large libraries; and long afterwards, Schopenhauer wrote that many people mistook the buying of a book for the buying of the contents of the book. Sometimes, looking at the many books I have at home, I feel I shall die before I come to the end of them, yet I cannot resist the temptation of buying new books. Whenever I walk into a bookstore and find a book on one of my hobbies—for example, Old English or Old Norse poetry—I say to myself, "What a pity I can't buy that book, for I already have a copy at home."

After the ancients, from the East there came a different idea of the book. There came the idea of Holy Writ, of books written by the Holy Ghost; there came Korans, Bibles, and so on. Following the example of Spengler in his *Untergang des Abendlandes—The Decline of the West*—I would like to take the Koran as an example. If I am not mistaken, Muslim theologians think of it as being prior to the creation of the word. The Koran is written in Arabic, yet Muslims think of it as being prior to the language. Indeed, I have read that they think of the Koran not as a work of God but as an attribute of God, even as His justice, His mercy, and His whole wisdom are.

And thus there came into Europe the idea of Holy Writ—an idea that is, I think, not wholly mistaken. Bernard Shaw (to whom I am always going back) was asked once whether he really thought the Bible was the work of the Holy Ghost. And he said, "I think the Holy Ghost has written not only the Bible, but all books." This is rather hard on the Holy Ghost, of course—but all books are worth reading, I suppose. This, I think, is what Homer meant when he spoke to the muse. And this is what the Hebrews and what Milton meant when they talked of the Holy Ghost whose temple is the upright and pure heart of men. And in our less beautiful mythology, we speak of the "subliminal self," of the "subconscious." Of course, these words are rather uncouth when we compare them to the muses or to the Holy Ghost. Still, we have to put up with the mythology of our time. For the words mean essentially the same thing.

We come now to the notion of the "classics." I must confess that I think a book is really not an immortal object to be picked up and duly worshiped, but rather an occasion for beauty. And it has to be so, for language is shifting all the time. I am very fond of etymologies and would like to recall to you (for I am sure you know much more about these things than I do) some rather curious etymologies.

For example, we have in English the verb "to tease"—a mischievous word. It means a kind of joke. Yet in Old English *tesan* meant "to wound with a sword," even as in French *navrer* meant "to thrust a sword through somebody." Then, to take a different Old English word, *þreat,* you may find out from the very first verses of *Beowulf* that it meant "an angry crowd"—that is to say, the cause of the "threat." And thus we might go on endlessly.

But now let us consider some particular verses. I take my examples from English, since I have a particular love for English literature—though my knowledge of it is, of course, limited. There are cases where poetry creates itself. For example, I don't think the words "quietus" and "bodkin" are especially beautiful; indeed, I would say they are rather uncouth. But if we think of "When he himself might his quietus make / With a bare bodkin," we are reminded of the great speech by Hamlet.[5] And thus the context creates poetry for those words—words that no one would ever dare to use nowadays, because they would be mere quotations.

Then there are other examples, and perhaps simpler ones. Let us take the title of one of the most famous books in the world, *Historia del ingenioso hidalgo Don Quijote de la Mancha.* The word *hidalgo* has today a peculiar dignity all its own, yet when Cervantes wrote it, the word *hidalgo* meant "a country gentleman." As for the name "Quixote," it was meant to be a rather ridiculous word, like the names of many of the characters in Dickens: Pickwick, Swiveller, Chuzzlewit, Twist, Squears, Quilp, and so on. And then you have "de la Mancha," which now sounds noble in Castilian to us, but when Cervantes wrote it down, he intended it to sound perhaps (I ask the apology of any resident of that city who may be here) as if he had written "Don Quixote of Kansas City." You see how those words have changed, how they have been ennobled. You see a strange fact: that because the old soldier Miguel de Cervantes poked mild fun at La Mancha, now "La Mancha" is one of the everlasting words of literature.

Let us take another example of verses that have changed. I am thinking of a sonnet by Rossetti, a sonnet that labors under the not-too-beautiful name "Inclusiveness." The sonnet begins thus:

> What man has bent o'er his son's sleep to brood,
> How that face shall watch his when cold it lies?—
> Or thought, as his own mother kissed his eyes,
> Of what her kiss was, when his father wooed?[6]

I think that these lines are perhaps more vivid now than when they were written, some eighty years ago, because the cinema has taught us to follow quick sequences of visual images. In the first line, "What man has bent o'er his son's sleep to brood," we have the father bending over the face of the sleeping son. And then in the second line, as in a good film, we have the same image reversed: we see the son bending over the face of that dead man, his father. And perhaps our recent study of psychology has made us more sensitive to these lines: "Or thought, as his own mother kissed his eyes, / Of what her kiss was, when his father wooed." Here we have, of course, the beauty of the soft English vowels in "brood," "wooed." And the additional beauty of "wooed" being by itself—not "wooed her" but simply "wooed." The word goes on ringing.

There is also a different kind of beauty. Let us take an adjective that once was commonplace. I have no Greek, but I think that the Greek is *oinopa pontos,* and the common English rendering is "the wine-dark sea." I suppose the word "dark" is slipped in to make things easier for the reader. Perhaps it would be "the winy sea," or something of the kind. I am sure that when Homer (or the many Greeks who recorded Homer) wrote it, they were simply thinking of the sea; the adjective was straightforward. But nowadays, if I or if any of you, after trying many fancy adjectives, write in a poem "the wine-dark sea," this is not a mere repetition of what the Greeks wrote. Rather, it is a going back to tradition. When we speak of "the wine-dark sea," we think of Homer and of the thirty centuries that lie between us and him. So that although the words may be much the same, when we write "the wine-dark sea" we are really writing something quite different from what Homer was writing.

Thus, the language is shifting; the Latins knew all about that. And the reader is shifting also. This brings us back to the old metaphor of the Greeks—the metaphor, or rather the truth, about no man stepping twice into the same river.[7] And there is, I think, an element of fear here. At first we are apt to think of the river as flowing. We think, "Of course, the river goes on but the water is changing." Then, with an emerging sense of awe, we feel that we too are changing—that we are as shifting and evanescent as the river is.

However, we need not worry too much about the fate of the classics, because beauty is always with us. Here I would like to quote another verse, by Browning, perhaps a now-forgotten poet. He says:

> Just when we're safest, there's a sunset-touch,
> A fancy from a flower-bell, some one's death,
> A chorus-ending from Euripides.[8]

Yet the first line is enough: "Just when we're safest . . ." That is to say, beauty is lurking all about us. It may come to us in the name of a film; it may come to us in some popular lyric; we may even find it in the pages of a great or famous writer.

And since I have spoken of a dead master of mine, Rafael Cansinos-Asséns (maybe this is the second time you've heard his name; I don't quite know why he is forgotten),[9] I remember that Cansinos-Asséns wrote a very fine prose poem wherein he asked God to defend him, to save him from beauty, because, he says, "there is too much beauty in the world." He thought that beauty was overwhelming it. Although I do not know if I have been a particularly happy man (I hope I am going to be happy at the ripe age of sixty-seven), I still think that beauty is all around us.

As to whether a poem has been written by a great poet or not, this is important only to historians of literature. Let us suppose, for the sake of argument, that I have written a beautiful line; let us take this as a working hypothesis. Once I have written it, that line does me no good, because, as I've already said, that line came to me from the Holy Ghost, from the subliminal self, or perhaps from some other writer. I often find I am merely quoting something I read some time ago, and then that becomes a rediscovering. Perhaps it is better that a poet should be nameless.

I spoke of "the wine-dark sea," and since my hobby is Old English (I am afraid that, if you have the courage or the patience to come back to some of my lectures, you may have more Old English inflicted on you), I would like to recall some lines that I think beautiful. I will say them first in English, and then in the stark and voweled Old English of the ninth century.

> It snowed from the north;
> rime bound the fields;
> hail fell on earth,
> the coldest of seeds.

> Norþan sniwde
> hrim hrusan bond
> hægl feol on eorþan
> corna caldast.[10]

This takes us back to what I said about Homer: when the poet wrote these lines, he was merely recording things that had happened. This was of course very strange in the ninth century, when people thought in terms of mythology, allegorical images, and so on. He was merely telling very commonplace things. But nowadays when we read

> It snowed from the north;
> rime bound the fields;
> hail fell on earth,
> the coldest of seeds . . .

there is an added poetry. There is the poetry of a nameless Saxon having written those lines by the shores of the North Sea—in Northumberland, I think; and of those lines coming to us so straightforward, so plain, and so pathetic through the centuries. So we have both cases: the case (I need hardly dwell upon it) when time debases a poem, when the words lose their beauty; and also the case when time enriches rather than debases a poem.

I talked at the beginning about definitions. To end up, I would like to say that we make a very common mistake when we think that we're ignorant of something because we are unable to define it. If we are in a Chestertonian mood (one of the very best moods to be in, I think), we might say that we can define something only when we know nothing about it.

For example, if I have to define poetry, and if I feel rather shaky about it, if I'm not too sure about it, I say something like: "Poetry is the expression of the beautiful through the medium of words artfully woven together." This definition may be good enough for a dictionary or for a textbook, but we all feel that it is rather feeble. There is something far more important—something that may encourage us to go on not only trying our hand at writing poetry, but enjoying it and feeling that we know all about it.

This is that we *know* what poetry is. We know it so well that we cannot define it in other words, even as we cannot define the taste of coffee, the color red or yellow, or the meaning of anger, of love, of hatred, of the sunrise, of the sunset, or of our love for our country. These things are so deep in us that they can be expressed only by those common symbols that we share. So why should we need other words?

You may not agree with the examples I have chosen. Perhaps tomorrow I may think of better examples, may think I might have quoted other lines. But as you can pick and choose your own examples, it is not needful that you care greatly about Homer, or about the Anglo-Saxon poets, or about Rossetti. Because everyone knows where to find poetry. And when it comes, one feels the touch of poetry, that particular tingling of poetry.

To end with, I have a quotation from Saint Augustine which comes in very fitly, I think. He said, "What is time? If people do not ask me what time is, I know. If they ask me what it is, then I do not know."[11] I feel the same way about poetry.

One is hardly troubled about definitions. This time I am rather at sea, because I am no good at all at abstract thinking. But in the following lectures—if you are good enough to put up with me—we will take more concrete examples. I will speak about the metaphor, about word-music, about the possibility or impossibility of verse translation, and about the telling of a tale—that is to say, about epic poetry, the oldest and perhaps the bravest kind of poetry. And I will end with something that I can hardly divine now. I will end with a lecture called "The Poet's Creed," wherein I will try to justify my own life and the confidence some of you may have in me, despite this rather awkward and fumbling first lecture of mine.

THE

METAPHOR

As the subject of today's talk is the metaphor, I shall begin with a metaphor. This first of the many metaphors I shall try to recall comes from the Far East, from China. If I am not mistaken, the Chinese call the world "the ten thousand things," or—and this depends on the taste and fancy of the translator—"the ten thousand beings."

We may accept, I suppose, the very conservative estimate of ten thousand. Surely there are more than ten thousand ants, ten thousand men, ten thousand hopes, fears, or nightmares in the world. But if we accept the number ten thousand, and if we think that all metaphors are made by linking two different things together, then, had we time enough, we might work out an almost unbelievable sum of possible meta-phors. I have forgotten my algebra, but I think that the sum should be 10,000 multiplied by 9,999, multi-plied by 9,998, and so on. Of course the sum of possible combinations is not endless, but it staggers the imagination. So we might be led to think: Why on earth should poets all over the world, and all through time, be using the same stock metaphors, when there are so many possible combinations?

The Argentine poet Lugones, way back in the year 1909, wrote that he thought poets were always using the same metaphors, and that he would try his hand at discovering new metaphors for the moon. And in fact he concocted many hundreds of them. He also said, in the foreword to a book called *Lunario sentimental*,[1] that every word is a dead metaphor. This statement is, of course, a metaphor. Yet I think we all feel the difference between dead and living metaphors. If we take any good etymological dictionary (I am thinking of my old unknown friend Dr. Skeat)[2] and if we look up any word, we are sure to find a metaphor tucked away somewhere.

For example—and you can find this in the very first lines of *Beowulf*—the word *þreat* meant "an angry mob," but now the word is given to the effect and not to the cause. Then we have the word "king." "King" was originally *cyning,* which meant "a man who stands for the kin—for the people." So, etymologically, "king," "kinsman," and "gentleman" are the same word. Yet if I say, "The king sat in his counting house, counting out his money," we don't think of the word "king" as being a metaphor. In fact, if we go in for abstract thinking, we have to forget that words were metaphors. We have to forget, for example, that in the word "consider" there is a suggestion of astrology—"consider" originally meaning "being with the stars," "making a horoscope."

What is important about the metaphor, I should say, is the fact of its being felt by the reader or the hearer *as* a metaphor. I will confine this talk to metaphors that *are* felt as metaphors by the reader. Not to such words as "king," or "threat"—and we might go on, perhaps forever.

First, I would like to take some stock patterns of metaphor. I use the word "pattern" because the metaphors I will quote will be to the imagination quite different, yet to the logical thinker they would be almost the same. So that we might speak of them as equations. Let us take the first that comes to my mind. Let us take the stock comparison, the time-honored comparison, of eyes and stars, or conversely of stars and eyes. The first example I remember comes from the Greek Anthology,[3] and I think Plato is supposed to have written it. The lines (I have no Greek) run more or less as follows: "I wish I were the night, so that I might watch your sleep with a thousand eyes." Here, of course, what we feel is the tenderness of the lover; we feel his wish to be able to see his beloved from many points at once. We feel the tenderness behind these lines.

Now let us take another, less illustrious example: "The stars look down." If we take logical thinking seriously, we have the same metaphor here. Yet the effect on our imagination is quite different. "The stars look down" does not make us think of tenderness; rather, it gives the idea of generations and generations of men toiling on and of the stars looking down with a kind of lofty indifference.

Let me take a different example—one of the stanzas that have most struck me. The lines come from a poem by Chesterton called "A Second Childhood":

> But I shall not grow too old to see enormous night
>   arise,
> A cloud that is larger than the world
> And a monster made of eyes.[4]

Not a monster *full* of eyes (we know those monsters from the Revelation of Saint John) but—and this is far more awful—a monster *made* of eyes, as if those eyes were the living tissue of him.

We have looked at three images which can all be traced back to the same pattern. But the point I would like to emphasize—and this is really one of the two important points in my talk—is that although the pattern is essentially the same, in the first case, the Greek example "I wish I were the night," what the poet makes us feel is his tenderness, his anxiety; in the second, we feel a kind of divine indifference to things human; and in the third, the familiar night becomes a nightmare.

Let us now take a different pattern: let us take the idea of time flowing—flowing as a river does. The first example comes from a poem that Tennyson wrote when he was, I think, thirteen or fourteen. He destroyed it; but, happily for us, one line survived. I think you will find it in Tennyson's biography written by Andrew Lang.[5] The line is: "Time flowing in the middle of the night." I think Tennyson has chosen his time very wisely. In the night all things are silent, men are sleeping, yet time is flowing noiselessly on. This is one example.

There is also a novel (I'm sure you're thinking of it) called simply *Of Time and the River*.[6] The mere putting together of the two words suggests the metaphor: time and the river, they both flow on. And then there is the famous sentence of the Greek philosopher: "No man steps twice into the same river."[7] Here we have the beginning of terror, because at first we think of the river as flowing on, of the drops of water as being different. And then we are made to feel that *we* are the river, that we are as fugitive as the river.

We also have those lines by Manrique:

> Nuestras vidas son los ríos
> que van a dar en la mar
> qu'es el morir.

> Our lives are the rivers
> that flow into that sea
> which is death.[8]

This statement is not too impressive in English; I wish I could remember how Longfellow translated it in his "Coplas de Manrique."[9] But of course (and we shall go into this question in another lecture) behind the stock metaphor we have the grave music of the words:

> Nuestras vidas son los ríos
> que van a dar en la mar

qu'es el morir;
allí van los señoríos
derechos a se acabar
e consumir . . .

Yet the metaphor is exactly the same in all these cases.

And now we will go on to something very trite, something that may cause you to smile: the comparison of women to flowers, and also of flowers to women. Here, of course, there are far too many easy examples. But there is one I would like to recall (perhaps it may not be familiar to you) from that unfinished masterwork, Robert Louis Stevenson's *Weir of Hermiston*. Stevenson tells of his hero going into a church, in Scotland, where he sees a girl—a lovely girl, we are made to feel. And one feels that he is about to fall in love with her. Because he looks at her, and then he wonders whether there is an immortal soul within that beautiful frame, or whether she is a mere animal the color of flowers. And the brutality of the word "animal" is of course destroyed by "the color of flowers." I don't think we need any other examples of this pattern, which can be found in all ages, in all tongues, in all literatures.

Now let us go on to another of the essential patterns of metaphor: the pattern of life's being a dream—the feeling that comes over us that life is a dream. The evident example which occurs to us is: "We are such stuff as dreams are made on."[10] Now, this may sound like blasphemy—I love Shakespeare too much to care—but I think that here, if we look at it (and I don't think we should look at it too closely; we should rather be grateful to Shakespeare for this and his many other gifts), there is a very slight contradiction between the fact that our lives are dreamlike or have a dreamlike essence in them, and the rather sweeping statement, "We are such stuff as dreams are made on." Because if we are real in dreams, or if we are merely dreamers of dreams, then I wonder if we can make such sweeping statements. This sentence of Shakespeare's belongs rather to philosophy or to metaphysics than to poetry—though of course it is heightened, it is lifted up into poetry, by the context.

Another example of the same pattern comes from a great German poet—a minor poet beside Shakespeare (but I suppose all poets are minor beside him, except two or three). It is a very famous piece by Walther von der Vogelweide. I suppose I should say it thus (I wonder how good my Middle German is— you will have to forgive me): "Ist mir mîn leben getroumet, oder ist es war?" "Have I dreamt my life, or was it a true one?"[11] I think this comes nearer to what the poet is trying to say, because instead of a sweeping affirmation we have a question. The poet is wondering. This has happened to all of us, but we have not worded it as Walther von der Vogelweide did. He is asking himself, "Ist mir mîn leben ge-troumet, oder ist es war?" and this hesitation gives us that dreamlike essence of life, I think.

I don't remember whether in my last lecture (because this is a sentence I often quote over and over again, and have quoted all through my life) I gave you the quotation from the Chinese philosopher Chuan Tzu. He dreamt that he was a butterfly, and, on wak-ing up, he did not know whether he was a man who had had a dream he was a butterfly, or a butterfly who was now dreaming he was a man. This metaphor is, I think, the finest of all. First because it begins with a dream, so afterwards, when he awakens, his life has still something dreamlike about it. And second be-cause, with a kind of almost miraculous happiness, he has chosen the right animal. Had he said, "Chuan Tzu had a dream that he was a tiger," then there would be nothing in it. A butterfly has something delicate and evanescent about it. If we are dreams, the true way to suggest this is with a butterfly and not a tiger. If

Chuan Tzu had a dream he was a typewriter, it would be no good at all. Or a whale—*that* would do him no good either. I think he has chosen just the right word for what he is trying to say.

Let us try to follow another pattern—the very common one that links up the ideas of sleeping and dying. This is quite common in everyday speech also; yet if we look for examples, we shall find that they are very different. I think that somewhere in Homer he speaks of the "iron sleep of death."[12] Here he gives us two opposite ideas: death is a kind of sleep, yet that kind of sleep is made of a hard, ruthless, and cruel metal—iron. It is a kind of sleep that is unbroken and unbreakable. Of course, we have Heine here also: "Der Tod daß ist die frühe Nacht." And since we are north of Boston, I think we must remember those perhaps too-well-known lines by Robert Frost:

> The woods are lovely, dark, and deep,
> But I have promises to keep,
> And miles to go before I sleep,
> And miles to go before I sleep.[13]

These lines are so perfect that we hardly think of a trick. Yet, unhappily, all literature is made of tricks, and those tricks get—in the long run—found out.

And then the reader tires of them. But in this case the trick is so unobtrusive that I feel rather ashamed of myself for calling it a trick (I call it this merely for want of a better word). Because Frost has attempted something very daring here. We have the same line repeated word for word, twice over, yet the sense is different. "And miles to go before I sleep": this is merely physical—the miles are miles in space, in New England, and "sleep" means "go to sleep." The second time—"And miles to go before I sleep"—we are made to feel that the miles are not only in space but in time, and that "sleep" means "die" or "rest." Had the poet said so in so many words, he would have been far less effective. Because, as I understand it, anything suggested is far more effective than anything laid down. Perhaps the human mind has a tendency to deny a statement. Remember what Emerson said: arguments convince nobody. They convince nobody because they are presented as arguments. Then we look at them, we weigh them, we turn them over, and we decide against them.

But when something is merely said or—better still—hinted at, there is a kind of hospitality in our imagination. We are ready to accept it. I remember reading, some thirty years ago, the works of Martin

Buber—I thought of them as being wonderful poems. Then, when I went to Buenos Aires, I read a book by a friend of mine, Dujovne,[14] and I found in its pages, much to my astonishment, that Martin Buber was a philosopher and that all his philosophy lay in the books I had read as poetry. Perhaps I had accepted those books because they came to me through poetry, through suggestion, through the music of poetry, and not as arguments. I think that somewhere in Walt Whitman the same idea can be found: the idea of reasons being unconvincing. I think he says somewhere that he finds the night air, the large few stars, far more convincing than mere arguments.

We may think of other patterns of metaphor. Let us now take the example (this is not as common as the other ones) of a battle and a fire. In the *Iliad,* we find the image of a battle blazing like a fire. We have the same idea in the heroic fragment of Finnesburg.[15] In that fragment we are told of the Danes fighting the Frisians, of the glitter of the weapons, the shields and swords, and so on. Then the writer says that it seemed as if all Finnesburg, as if the whole castle of Finn, were on fire.

I suppose I have left out some quite common patterns. We have so far taken up eyes and stars, women and flowers, time and rivers, life and dream, death and sleeping, fire and battles. Had we time and learning enough, we might find half a dozen other patterns, and perhaps those might give us most of the metaphors in literature.

What is really important is the fact not that there are a few patterns, but that those patterns are capable of almost endless variations. The reader who cares for poetry and not for the theory of poetry might read, for example, "I wish I were the night," and then afterwards "A monster made of eyes" or "The stars looked down," and never stop to think that these can be traced back to a single pattern. If I were a daring thinker (but I am not; I am a very timid thinker, I am groping my way along), I could of course say that only a dozen or so patterns exist and that all other metaphors are mere arbitrary games. This would amount to the statement that among the "ten thousand things" of the Chinese definition, only some twelve essential affinities may be found. Because, of course, you can find other affinities that are merely astonishing, and astonishment hardly lasts more than a moment.

I remember that I have forgotten quite a good example of the dream-and-life equation. But I think I can recall it now: it is by the American poet Cummings.

There are four lines. I must apologize for the first. Evidently it was written by a young man, writing for young men, and I can no longer claim the privilege—I am far too old for that kind of game. But the stanza should be quoted in full. The first line is: "god's terrible face, brighter than a spoon." I am rather sorry about the spoon, because of course one feels that he thought at first of a sword, or of a candle, or of the sun, or of a shield, or of something traditionally shining; and then he said, "No—after all, I'm modern, so I'll work in a spoon." And so he got his spoon. But we may forgive him that for what comes afterwards: "god's terrible face, brighter than a spoon, / collects the image of one fatal word." This second line is better, I think. And as my friend Murchison said to me, in a spoon we often have many images collected. I had never thought of that, because I had been taken aback by the spoon and did not want to think much about it.

> god's terrible face, brighter than a spoon,
> collects the image of one fatal word,
> so that my life (which liked the sun and the moon)
> resembles something that has not occurred.[16]

"Resembles something that has not occurred": this line carries a kind of strange simplicity. I think it gives us the dreamlike essence of life better than those more famous poets, Shakespeare and Walther von der Vogelweide.

Of course, I have chosen only a few examples. I am sure your memories are full of metaphors that you have treasured up—metaphors that you may be hoping I will quote. I know that after this lecture I shall feel remorse coming over me, thinking of the many beautiful metaphors I have missed. And of course you will say to me, in an aside, "But why did you omit that wonderful metaphor by So-and-So?" And then I will have to fumble and to apologize.

But now, I think, we might go on to metaphors that seem to stand outside the old patterns. And since I have spoken of the moon, I will take a Persian metaphor I read somewhere in Brown's history of Persian literature. Let us say it came from Farid al-Din Attar or Omar Khayyám, or Hafiz,[17] or another of the great Persian poets. He speaks of the moon, calling it "the mirror of time." I suppose that, from the point of view of astronomy, the idea of the moon being a mirror is as it should be—but this is quite irrelevant from the poetic point of view. Whether in fact the moon is or is not a mirror has no importance whatever, since poetry speaks to the imagination. Let us look at the moon as a mirror of time. I think this is a very fine metaphor—first, because the idea of a mirror gives us the brightness and the fragility of the moon, and, second, because the idea of time makes us suddenly remember that that very clear moon we are looking at is very ancient, is full of poetry and mythology, is as old as time.

Since I've used the phrase "as old as time," I must quote another line—one that perhaps is bubbling up in your memory. I can't recall the name of the author. I found it quoted by Kipling in a not-too-memorable book of his called *From Sea to Sea:* "A rose-red city, half as old as Time."[18] Had the poet written "A rose-red city, as old as Time," he would have written nothing at all. But "half as old as Time" gives it a kind of magic precision—the same kind of magic precision that is achieved by that strange and common English phrase, "I will love you forever and a day." "Forever" means "a very long time," but it is too abstract to appeal to the imagination.

We have the same kind of trick (I apologize for the use of this word) in the name of that famous book, the *Thousand and One Nights.* For "the thousand nights" means to the imagination "the many nights," even as "forty" used to mean "many" in the seventeenth century. "When forty winters shall besiege thy brow," writes Shakespeare;[19] and I think of the common English expression "forty winks" for "a nap." For "forty" means "many." And here you have the "thousand nights and a night"—like "a rose-red city" and the fanciful precision of "half as old as Time," which of course makes time seem even longer.

In order to consider different metaphors, I will now go back—inevitably, you might say—to my favorite Anglo-Saxons. I remember that very common *kenning*[20] which calls the sea "the whale road." I wonder whether the unknown Saxon who first coined that *kenning* knew how fine it was. I wonder whether he felt (though this need hardly concern us) that the hugeness of the whale suggested and emphasized the hugeness of the sea.

There is another metaphor—a Norse one, about blood. The common *kenning* for blood is "the water of the serpent." In this metaphor, you have the notion—which we find also among the Saxons—of a sword as an essentially evil being, a being that lapped up the blood of men as if it were water.

Then we have the metaphors for battle. Some of them are quite trite—for example, "meeting of men." Here, perhaps, there is something quite fine: the idea of men meeting to kill each other (as if no other "meetings" were possible). But we also have "the meeting of swords," "the dance of swords," "the clash of armor," "the clash of shields." All of them may be found in the "Ode" of Brunanburh. And there is another fine one: *þorn æneoht,* "a meeting of anger." Here the metaphor is impressive perhaps because, when we think of meeting, we think of fellowship, of friendship; and then there comes the contrast, the meeting of *anger.*

But these metaphors are nothing, I should say, compared to a very fine Norse and—strangely enough—Irish metaphor about the battle. It calls the battle "the web of men." The word "web" is really wonderful here, for in the idea of a web we get the pattern of a medieval battle: we have the swords, the shields, the crossing of the weapons. Also, there is the nightmare touch of a web being made of living beings. "A web of men": a web of men who are dying and killing each other.

There suddenly comes to my mind a metaphor from Góngora that is rather like the "web of men." He is speaking of a traveler who comes to a "bárbara aldea"—to a "barbarous village"; and then that village weaves a rope of dogs around him.

Como suele tejer
Bárbara aldea
Soga de perros
Contra forastero.

So, strangely enough, we have the same image: the idea of a rope or web made of living beings. Yet even in those cases that seem to be synonyms, there is quite a difference. A rope of dogs is somehow baroque and grotesque, while "web of men" has something terrible, something awful about it.

To end up, I will take a metaphor, or a comparison (after all, I am not a professor and the difference need hardly worry me), by the now-forgotten Byron. I read the poem when I was a boy—I suppose you all read it at a very tender age. Yet two or three days ago I suddenly discovered that that metaphor was a very complex one. I had never thought of Byron as being especially complex. You all know the words: "She walks in beauty, like the night."[21] The line is so perfect that we take it for granted. We think, "Well, *we* could have written that, had we cared to." But only Byron cared to write it.

I come now to the hidden and secret complexity of the line. I suppose you have already found out what I am now going to reveal to you. (Because this always happens with surprises, no? It happens to us when we're reading a detective novel.) "She walks in beauty, like the night": at the beginning we have a lovely woman; then we are told that she walks in beauty. This somehow suggests the French language—something like "vous êtes en beauté," and so on. But: "She walks in beauty, like the night." We have, in the first instance, a lovely woman, a lovely lady, likened to the night. But in order to understand the line, we have to think of the night as a woman also; if not, the line is meaningless. So within those very simple words, we have a double metaphor: a woman is likened to the night, but the night is likened to a woman. I do not know and I do not care whether Byron knew this. I think if he *had* known it, the verse would hardly be as good as it is. Perhaps before he died he found it out, or somebody pointed it out to him.

Now we are led to the two obvious and major conclusions of this lecture. The first is, of course, that though there are hundreds and indeed thousands of metaphors to be found, they may all be traced back to a few simple patterns. But this need not trouble us, since each metaphor is different: every time the pattern is used, the variations are different. And the second conclusion is that there are metaphors—for example, "web of men," or "whale road"—that may not be traced back to definite patterns.

So I think that the outlook—even after my lecture—is quite good for the metaphor. Because, if we like, we may try our hand at new variations of the major trends. The variations would be very beautiful, and only a few critics like myself would take the trouble to say, "Well, there you have eyes and stars and there you have time and the river over and over again." The metaphors will strike the imagination. But it may also be given to us—and why not hope for this as well?—it may also be given to us to invent metaphors that do not belong, or that do not yet belong, to accepted patterns.

Verbal distinctions should be valued, since they stand for mental—intellectual—distinctions. Yet one feels it is somehow a pity that the word "poet" should have been split asunder. For nowadays when we speak of a poet, we think only of the utterer of such lyric, birdlike notes as "With ships the sea was sprinkled far and nigh, / Like stars in heaven" (Wordsworth),[1] or "Music to hear, why hear'st thou music sadly? / Sweets with sweets war not, joy delights in joy."[2] Whereas the ancients, when they spoke of a poet—a "maker"—thought of him not only as the utterer of those high lyric notes, but also as the teller of a tale. A tale wherein all the voices of mankind might be found—not only the lyric, the wistful, the melancholy, but also the voices of courage and of hope. This means that I am speaking of what I suppose is the oldest form of poetry: the epic. Let us consider a few of them.

Perhaps the first which comes to our mind is the one that Andrew Lang, who so finely translated it, called *The Tale of Troy*. We will look into it for that very ancient telling of a tale. In the very first line, we have something like: "Tell me, muse, of the anger of Achilles." Or, as Professor Rouse, I think, has translated it: "An angry man—that is my subject."[3] Perhaps Homer, or the man we call Homer (for that is an old question, of course), thought he was writing his poem about an angry man, and this somehow disconcerts us. For we think of anger as the Latins did: "ira furor brevis"—anger is a brief madness, a fit of madness. The plot of the *Iliad* is really, in itself, not a charming one—the idea of the hero sulking in his tent, feeling that the king has dealt unjustly with him, and then taking up the war as a private feud because his friend has been killed, and afterwards selling the dead man he has killed to the man's father.

But perhaps (I may have said this before; I am sure I have), perhaps the intentions of the poet are not that important. What is important nowadays is that although Homer might have thought he was telling that story, he was actually telling something far finer: the story of a man, a hero, who is attacking a city he knows he will never conquer, who knows he will die before it falls; and the still more stirring tale of men defending a city whose doom is already known to them, a city that is already in flames. I think this is the real subject of the *Iliad*. And, in fact, men have always felt that the Trojans were the real heroes. We think of Virgil, but we may also think of Snorri Sturluson,[4] who, in his younger era, wrote that Odin—the Odin of the Saxons, the god—was the son of Priam and the brother of Hector. Men have sought kinship with the defeated Trojans, and not with the victorious Greeks. This is perhaps because there is a dignity in defeat that hardly belongs to victory.

Let us take a second epic, the *Odyssey*. The *Odyssey* may be read in two ways. I suppose the man (or the woman, as Samuel Butler thought)[5] who had written it felt that there were really two stories: the homecoming of Ulysses, and the marvels and perils of the sea. If we take the *Odyssey* in the first sense, then we have the idea of homecoming, the idea that we are in banishment, that our true home is in the past or in heaven or somewhere else, that we are never at home.

But of course the seafaring and the homecoming had to be made interesting. So the many marvels were worked in. And already, when we come to the *Arabian Nights,* we find that the Arabian version of the *Odyssey,* the *Seven Voyages of Sindbad the Sailor,* is not a story of homecoming but a story of adventure; and I think we read it thus. When we read the *Odyssey,* I think that what we feel is the glamour, the magic of the sea; what we feel is what we find in the seafarer. For example, he has no heart for the harp, nor for the giving of rings, nor for the delight of a woman, nor for the greatness of the world. He thinks only of the long sea salt streams. So that we have both stories in one: we can read it as a homecoming, and we can read it as a tale of adventure—perhaps the finest that has ever been written or sung.

We come now to a third "poem" that looms far above them: the four Gospels. The Gospels may also be read in two ways. By the believer, they are read as the strange story of a man, of a god, who atones for the sins of mankind. A god who condescends to suffering—to death on the "bitter cross," as Shakespeare has it.[6] There is a still stranger interpretation, which I found in Langland:[7] the idea that God wanted to know all about human suffering, and that it was not enough for Him to know it intellectually, as a god might; he wanted to suffer as a man, and with the limitations of a man. However, if you are an unbeliever (many of us are) then you can read the story in a different way. You can think of a man of genius, of a man who thought he was a god and who at the end found out that he was merely a man, and that god—his god—had forsaken him.

It might be said that for many centuries, those three stories—the tale of Troy, the tale of Ulysses, the tale of Jesus—have been sufficient for mankind. People have been telling and retelling them over and over again; they have been set to music; they have been painted. People have told them many times over, yet the stories are still there, illimitable. You might think of somebody, in a thousand years or ten thousand years, writing them over again. But in the case of the Gospels, there is a difference: the story of Christ, I think, cannot be told better. It has been told many times over, yet I think the few verses where we read, for example, of Christ being tempted by Satan are stronger than all four books of *Paradise Regained*. One feels that Milton perhaps had no inkling as to what kind of a man Christ was.

Well, we have these stories and we have the fact

that men did not need many stories. I don't suppose Chaucer ever thought of inventing a story. I don't think people were less inventive in those days than they are today. I think they felt that the new shadings brought into the story—the fine shadings brought into it—were enough. Besides, it made things easier for the poet. His hearers or his readers knew what he was going to say. And so they could take in all the differences.

Now, in the epic—and we might think of the Gospels as a kind of divine epic—all things could be found. But poetry, as I said, has fallen asunder; or rather, on the one hand we have the lyrical poem and the elegy, and on the other we have the telling of a tale—we have the novel. One is almost tempted to think of the novel as a degeneration of the epic, in spite of such writers as Joseph Conrad or Herman Melville. For the novel goes back to the dignity of the epic.

If we think of the novel and the epic, we are tempted to fall into thinking that the chief difference lies in the difference between verse and prose, in the difference between singing something and stating something. But I think there is a greater difference. The difference lies in the fact that the important thing about the epic is a hero—a man who is a pattern for all men. While, as Mencken pointed out, the essence of most novels lies in the breaking down of a man, in the degeneration of character.

This brings us to another question: What do we think of happiness? What do we think of defeat, and of victory? Nowadays when people talk of a happy ending, they think of it as a mere pandering to the public, or they think it is a commercial device; they think of it as artificial. Yet for centuries men could very sincerely believe in happiness and in victory, though they felt the essential dignity of defeat. For example, when people wrote about the Golden Fleece (one of the ancient stories of mankind), readers and hearers were made to feel from the beginning that the treasure would be found at the end.

Well, nowadays if an adventure is attempted, we know that it will end in failure. When we read—I think of an example I admire—*The Aspern Papers,*[8] we know that the papers will never be found. When we read Franz Kafka's *The Castle,* we know that the man will never get inside the castle. That is to say, we cannot really believe in happiness and in success. And this may be one of the poverties of our time. I suppose Kafka felt much the same when he wanted his books to be destroyed: he really wanted to write a happy and victorious book, and he felt that he could not do it. He might have written it, of course, but people would have felt that he was not telling the truth. Not the truth of facts but the truth of his dreams.

At the end of the eighteenth or the beginning of the nineteenth century, let's say (we need hardly go into a discussion of dates), man began to invent stories. Perhaps one might say that the attempt began with Hawthorne and with Edgar Allan Poe, but of course there are always forerunners. As Rubén Darío pointed out, nobody is the literary Adam. Still, it was Poe who wrote that a story should be written for the sake of the last sentence, and a poem for the sake of the last line. This degenerated into the trick story, and in the nineteenth and twentieth centuries people have invented all kinds of plots. Those plots are sometimes very clever. Those plots, if merely told, are cleverer than the plots of the epics. Yet somehow we feel that there is something artificial about them—or rather, that there is something trivial about them. If we take two cases—let us suppose the story of Dr. Jekyll and Mr. Hyde, then a novel or a film like *Psycho*—perhaps the plot of the second is cleverer, but we feel that there is more behind Stevenson's plot.

idea of the story being told by different characters—all those are leading to the moment when we shall feel that the novel is no longer with us.

But there is something about a tale, a story, that will be always going on. I do not believe men will ever tire of telling or hearing stories. And if along with the pleasure of being told a story we get the additional pleasure of the dignity of verse, then something great will have happened. Maybe I am an old-fashioned man from the nineteenth century, but I have optimism, I have hope; and as the future holds many things—as the future, perhaps, holds all things—I think the epic will come back to us. I believe that the poet shall once again be a maker. I mean, he will tell a story and he will also sing it. And we will not think of those two things as different, even as we do not think they are different in Homer or in Virgil.

For the sake of clarity, I shall confine myself now to the problem of verse translation. A minor problem but also a very relevant one. This discussion should pave us a way to the topic of word-music (or perhaps word-magic), of sense and sound in poetry.

According to a widely held superstition, all translations betray their matchless originals. This is expressed by the too-well-known Italian pun, "Traduttore, traditore," which is supposed to be unanswerable. Since this pun is very popular, there must be a kernel of truth, a core of truth, hidden somewhere in it.

We will go into a discussion of the possibilities (or otherwise) and the success (or otherwise) of verse translation. According to my habit, we will begin with a few examples, for I do not think that any discussion can be carried on without examples. Since my memory is sometimes quite akin to oblivion, I should choose brief examples. It would be beyond our time and my capacity to analyze whole stanzas or poems.

We will begin with the Ode of Brunanburh and Tennyson's translation of it. This ode (my dates are always rather shaky) was composed at the beginning of the tenth century to celebrate the victory of the Wessex men against the Dublin Vikings, the Scotsmen, and the Welsh. Let us go into the examination of a line or so. In the original, we find something that runs more or less like this: "sunne up æt morgentid mære tungol." That is to say, "the sun at morning-tide" or "at morning-time," and then "that famous star" or "that mighty star"—but here "famous" would be a better translation ("mære tungol"). The poet goes on to speak of the sun as "godes candel beorht"—"a bright candle of God."

This ode was done into English prose by Tennyson's son; it was published in a magazine.[1] The son probably explained to his father some essentials of the rules of Old English verse—about its beat, its use of alliteration instead of rhyme, and so on. Then Tennyson, who was very fond of experiments, tried his hand at writing Old English verse in modern English. It is noteworthy to remark that, although the experiment was quite successful, he never came back to it again. So if we were looking for Old English verse in Lord Alfred Tennyson's works, we would have to be content with that one outstanding example, the Ode of Brunanburh.

Those two fragments—"the sun, that famous star" and "the sun, the bright candle of God" ("godes candel beorht")—came to be translated by Tennyson thus: "when first the great / Sun-star of morning-tide."[2] Now, "sun-star of morning-tide" is, I think, a very striking translation. It is even more Saxon than the original, since we have two compound Germanic words: "sun-star" and "morning-tide." And of course, though "morning-tide" can be easily explained as "morning-time," we may also think that Tennyson wanted to suggest to us the image of the dawn as overflowing the sky. So what we have is a very strange phrase: "when first the great / Sun-star of morning-tide." And then a line later, when Tennyson comes to the "bright candle of God," he translates it as "Lamp of the Lord God."

Let us now take another example, not only a blameless but also a fine translation. This time we will consider a translation from the Spanish. It is the wonderful poem "Noche oscura del alma," "Dark Night of the Soul," written in the sixteenth century by one of the greatest—we may safely say *the* greatest—of Spanish poets, of all men who have used the Spanish language for the purposes of poetry. I am speaking, of course, of San Juan de la Cruz. The first stanza runs thus:

> En una noche oscura
> con ansias en amores inflamada
> ¡o dichosa ventura!
> salí sin ser notada
> estando ya mi casa sosegada.[3]

This is a wonderful stanza. But if we consider the last line torn from its context and taken by itself (to be sure, we are not allowed to do that), it is an undistinguished line: "estando ya mi casa sosegada," "when my house was quiet." We have the rather hissing sound of the three *s*'s in "casa sosegada." And "sosegada" is hardly a striking word. I am not trying to disparage the text. I am merely pointing out (and in a short time you will see why I am doing this) that the line taken by itself, torn from its context, is quite unremarkable.

This poem was translated into English by Arthur Symons at the end of the nineteenth century. The translation is not a good one, but if you care to look at it, you can find it in Yeats's *Oxford Book of Modern Verse*.[4] Some years ago a great Scottish poet who is also a South African, Roy Campbell, attempted a translation of "Dark Night of the Soul." I wish I had the book by me; but we will confine ourselves to the line I have just quoted, "estando ya mi casa sosegada," and we will see what Roy Campbell made of it. He translated it thus: "When all the house was hushed."[5] Here we have the word "all," which gives a sense of space, a sense of vastness, to the line. And then the beautiful, the lovely English word "hushed." "Hushed" seems to give us somehow the very music of silence.

I will add to these two very favorable examples of the art of translation a third one. This I will not discuss, since it is a case not of verse rendered into verse but rather of prose being lifted up into verse, into poetry. We have that common Latin tag (done from the Greek, of course), "Ars longa, vita brevis"—or, as I suppose we ought to pronounce it, "wita brewis." (This is certainly very ugly. Let us go back to "vita brevis"—to "Virgil" and not to "Wirgilius.") Here we have a plain statement, a statement of opinion. This is quite plain sailing; this is straightforward. It strikes no deep chord. In fact, it is a kind of prophecy of the telegram and of the literature evolved by it. "Art is long, life is short." This tag was repeated ever so many times. Then, in the fourteenth century, "un grand translateur,"[6] "a great translator"—Master Geoffrey Chaucer—needed that line. Of course, he wasn't thinking about medicine; he was thinking perhaps about poetry. But perhaps (I don't have the text with me, so we can choose), perhaps he was thinking of love and wanted to work in that line. He wrote: "The life so short, the craft so long to learn"—or, as you may suppose he pronounced it, "The lyf so short, the craft so long to lerne."[7] Here we get not only the statement but also the very music of wistfulness. We can see that the poet is not merely thinking of the arduous art and of the brevity of life; he is also feeling it. This is given by the apparently invisible, inaudible keyword—the word "so." "The lyf *so* short, the craft *so* long to lerne."

Let us go back to the first two examples: the famous Ode of Brunanburh and Tennyson, and the "Noche oscura del alma" of San Juan de la Cruz. If we consider the two translations I have quoted, they are not inferior to the original, yet we feel that there is a difference. The difference is beyond what the translator can do; it depends, rather, on the way we read poetry. For if we look back on the Ode of Brunanburh, we know that it came from deep emotion. We know that the Saxons had been beaten many times over by the Danes, and that they hated this. And we must think of the joy the West Saxons felt when, after a long day's struggle—the battle of Brunanburh, one of the greatest battles in the medieval history of England—they defeated Olaf, the king of the Dublin Vikings, and the hated Scotsmen and Welshmen. We think of what they felt; we think of the man who wrote the ode. Perhaps he was a monk. But the fact remains that instead of thanking God (in the orthodox fashion), he thanked the sword of his king and the sword of Prince Edmund for the victory. He does not say that God vouchsafed the victory to them; he says that they won it "swordda edgiou"—"by the edge of their swords." The whole poem is filled with a fierce, ruthless joy. He mocks those who have been defeated. He is very happy that they have been defeated. He talks of the king and his brother going back to their own Wessex—to their own "West-Saxonland," as Tennyson has it (each "went to his own West-Saxonland, glad of the war").[8] After that, he goes far back into English history; he thinks of the men who came over from Jutland, of Hengist and Horsa.[9] This is very strange—I do not suppose many men had that historical sense in the Middle Ages. So we have to think of the poem as coming out of deep emotion. We have to think of it as an onrush of great verse.

When we come to Tennyson's version, much as we may admire it (and I knew it before I knew the Saxon original), we think of it as a successful experiment in Old English verse wrought by a master of modern English verse; that is to say, the context is different. Of course, the translator is not to be blamed for this. The same thing happens in the case of San Juan de la Cruz and Roy Campbell: we may think (as I suppose we are allowed to think) that "when all the house was hushed" is verbally—from the point of view of mere literature—superior to "estando ya mi casa sosegada." But that is of no avail as regards our judgment of the two pieces, the Spanish original and the English rendering. In the first case, San Juan de la Cruz, we think that he reached the highest experience of which the soul of a man is capable—the experience of ecstasies, the blending together of a human soul with the soul of divinity, with the soul of the godhead, of God. After he had had that unutterable experience, he had to communicate it somehow in metaphors. Then he found ready to hand the "Song of Songs," and he took (many mystics have done this) he took the image of sexual love as an image for mystical union between man and his god, and he wrote the poem. Thus, we are hearing—we are overhearing, we may say, as in the case of the Saxon—the very words that he uttered.

Then we come to Roy Campbell's translation. We find it good, but we are perhaps apt to think, "Well, the Scotsman made, after all, quite a good job of it." This, of course, is different. That is to say, the difference between a translation and the original is not a difference in the texts themselves. I suppose if we did not know which was the original and which was the translation, we could judge them fairly. But, unhappily, we cannot do this. And so the translator's work is always supposed to be inferior—or, what is worse, is *felt* to be inferior—even though, verbally, the rendering may be as good as the text.

Now we come to another problem: the problem of literal translation. When I speak of "literal" translations, I am using a wide metaphor, since, if a translation cannot be true word for word to the original, it can still less be true letter for letter. In the nineteenth

century, a quite forgotten Greek scholar, Newman, attempted a literal hexameter translation of Homer.[10] It
was his purpose to publish a translation "against"
Pope's Homer. He used phrases such as "wet waves,"
"wine-dark sea," and so on. Now, Matthew Arnold
had his own theories on translating Homer. When
Mr. Newman's book came out, he reviewed it. Newman answered him; Matthew Arnold answered him
back. We can read that very lively and very intelligent
discussion in the essays of Matthew Arnold.

Both men had much to say on the two sides of the
question. Newman supposed that literal translation
was the most faithful one. Matthew Arnold began
with a theory about Homer. He said that in Homer
several qualities were to be found—clarity, nobility,
simplicity, and so on. He thought that a translator
should always convey the impression of those qualities, even when the text did not bear them out. Matthew Arnold pointed out that a literal translation
made for oddity and for uncouthness.

For example, in the Romance languages we do not
say "It is cold"—we say "It makes cold": "Il fait
froid," "Fa freddo," "Hace frío," and so on. Yet I
don't think anybody should translate "Il fait froid" by
"It makes cold." Another example: in English one

says "Good morning," and in Spanish one says "Buenos días" ("Good days"). If "Good morning" were translated as "Buena mañana," we should feel that this was a literal translation but hardly a true one.

Matthew Arnold pointed out that if a text be translated literally, then false emphases are created. I do not know whether he came across Captain Burton's translation of the *Arabian Nights;* perhaps he did so too late. For Burton translates *Quitab alif laila wa laila* as *Book of the Thousand Nights and a Night,* instead of *Book of the Thousand and One Nights.* This translation is a literal one. It is true word for word to the Arabic. Yet it is false in the sense that the words "book of the thousand nights and a night" are a common form in Arabic, while in English we have a slight shock of surprise. And this, of course, has not been intended by the original.

Matthew Arnold advised the translator of Homer to have a Bible at his elbow. He said that the Bible in English might be a kind of standard for a translation of Homer. Yet if Matthew Arnold had looked closely into his Bible, he might have seen that the English Bible is full of literal translations, and that part of the great beauty of the English Bible lies in those literal translations.

For example, in the English Bible we have "a tower of strength." This is the phrase translated, as supposed, by Luther as "ein feste Burg"—"a mighty (or a firm) stronghold." Then we have "the song of songs." I read in Fray Luis de León that the Hebrews had no superlatives, so they could not say "the highest song" or "the best song." They said "the song of songs," even as they might have said "the king of kings" for "the emperor" or "the highest king"; or "the moon of moons" for "the highest moon"; or "the night of nights" for the most hallowed of nights. If we compare the English rendering "song of songs" to the German by Luther, we see that Luther, who had no care for beauty, who merely wanted Germans to understand the text, translated it as "das hohe Lied," "the high lay." So we find that these two literal translations make for beauty.

In fact, it might be said that literal translations make not only, as Matthew Arnold pointed out, for uncouthness and oddity, but also for strangeness and beauty. This, I think, is felt by all of us; for if we look into a literal version of some outlandish poem, we expect something strange. If we do not find it, we feel somehow disappointed.

Now we come to one of the finest and most famous

English translations. I am speaking, of course, of Fitz-Gerald's *Rubáiyát* by Omar Khayyám.[11] The first stanza runs thus:

> Awake! For morning in the bowl of night
> Has flung the stone that puts the stars to flight;
> And, lo! the hunter of the East has caught
> The Sultan's turret in a daze of light.

As we know, the book was discovered in a bookstore by Swinburne and Rossetti. They were overwhelmed by its beauty. They knew nothing whatsoever of Edward FitzGerald, a quite unknown man of letters. He had tried his hand at translating Calderón, and Farid al-Din Attar's *Parliament of Birds;* these books were not too good. And then there came this famous book, now a classic.

Rossetti and Swinburne felt the beauty of the translation, yet we wonder if they would have felt this beauty had FitzGerald presented the *Rubáiyát* as an original (partly it *was* original) rather than as a translation. Would they think FitzGerald should have been allowed to say, "Awake! For morning in the bowl of night / Has flung the stone that puts the stars to flight"? (The second line sends us to a footnote, which explains that to fling a stone into a bowl is the sign for the departing of the caravan.) And I wonder if FitzGerald would have been allowed the "noose of light" and the "sultan's turret" in a poem of his own.

But I think that we can safely dwell on a single line—a line which is to be found in one of the other stanzas:

> Dreaming when dawn's left hand was in the sky
> I heard a voice within the tavern cry,
> "Awake my little ones, and fill the cup
> Before life's liquor in its cup be dry."

Let us dwell on the first line: "Dreaming when dawn's left hand was in the sky." Of course, the keyword in this line is the word "left." Had any other adjective been used, the line would have been meaningless. But "left hand" makes us think of something strange, of something sinister. We know that the right hand is associated with "right"—in other words with "righteousness," with "direct," and so on—while here we have the ominous word "left." Let us remember the Spanish phrase "lanzada de modo izquierdo que atraviese el corazón," ("launched leftwards to cross through the heart")—the idea of something sinister. We feel that there is something subtly wrong about "dawn's left hand." If the Persian was dreaming when dawn's left hand was in the sky, then his dream could become a nightmare at any moment. And of this we are slightly aware; we don't have to dwell on the word "left." For the word "left" makes all the difference—so delicate and so mysterious is the art of verse. We accept "Dreaming when dawn's left hand was in the sky" because we suppose that there is a Persian original behind it. As far as I am aware, Omar Khayyám does not bear FitzGerald out. This brings us to an interesting problem: a literal translation has created a beauty all its own.

I have always wondered about the origin of literal translations. Nowadays we are fond of literal translations; in fact, many of us accept only literal translations, because we want to give every man his due. That would have seemed a *crime* to translators in ages past. They were thinking of something far worthier. They wanted to prove that the vernacular was as capable of a great poem as the original. And I suppose that Don Juan de Jáuregui when he rendered Lucan into Spanish, thought of that also. I don't think any contemporary of Pope thought about Homer *and* Pope. I suppose that readers, the best readers anyhow, thought of the poem in itself. They were interested in the *Iliad* and in the *Odyssey,* and they had no care for verbal trifles. All throughout the Middle Ages, people thought of translation not in terms of a literal rendering but in terms of something being re-created. Of a poet's having read a work and then somehow evolving that work from himself, from his own might, from the possibilities hitherto known of his language.

How did literal translations begin? I do not think they came out of scholarship; I do not think they came out of scruples. I think they had a theological origin. For although people thought of Homer as the greatest of poets, still they knew that Homer was human ("quandoque dormitat bonus Homerus," and so on),[12] and so they could reshape his words. But when it came to translating the Bible, that was something quite different, because the Bible was supposed to have been written by the Holy Ghost. If we think of the Holy Ghost, if we think of the infinite intelligence of God undertaking a literary task, then we are not allowed to think of any chance elements—of any haphazard elements—in his work. No—if God writes a book, if God condescends to literature, then every word, every letter, as the Kabbalists said, must have been thought out. And it might be blasphemy to tamper with the text written by an endless, eternal intelligence.

Thus, I think the idea of a literal translation came from translations of the Bible. This is merely my guess (I suppose there are many scholars here who can correct me if I make a mistake), but I think it is highly probable. When very fine translations of the Bible were undertaken, men began to discover, began to feel, that there was a beauty in alien ways of expression. Now everybody is fond of literal translations because a literal translation always gives us those small jolts of surprise that we expect. In fact, it might be said that no original is needed. Perhaps a time will come when a translation will be considered as something in itself. We may think of Elizabeth Barrett Browning's *Sonnets from the Portuguese.*

Sometimes I have attempted a rather bold metaphor, but have seen that no one would accept it if it came from me (I am a mere contemporary), and so I have attributed it to some out-of-the-way Persian or Norseman. Then my friends have said that it was quite fine; and of course I have never told them that I invented it, because I was fond of the metaphor. After all, the Persians or Norsemen *may* have invented that metaphor, or far better ones.

Thus, we go back to what I said at the beginning: that a translation is never judged verbally. It should be judged verbally, but it never is. For example (and I hope you won't think that I am uttering a blasphemy), I have looked very carefully (but that was forty years ago, and I can plead the mistakes of youth) into Baudelaire's *Fleurs du mal* and into Stefan George's *Blumen des Böse.* I think that of course Baudelaire was a greater poet than Stefan George, but Stefan George was a far more skillful craftsman. I think that if we compare them line by line, we should find that Stefan George's *Umdichtung* (this is a fine German word that means not a poem translated from another, but a poem woven around another; we also have *Nachdichtung,* an "after-poem," a translation; and *Übersetzung,* a mere translation)—I think that Stefan George's translation is perhaps better than Baudelaire's book. But of course this will do Stefan George no good, since people who are interested in Baudelaire—and I have been very much interested in Baudelaire—think of his words as coming from him; that is to say, they think of the context of his whole life. While in the case of Stefan George we have an efficient but rather priggish twentieth-century poet turning Baudelaire's very words into an alien language, into German.

I have spoken of the present. I say that we are burdened, overburdened, by our historical sense. We cannot look into an ancient text as the men of the Middle Ages or the Renaissance or even the eighteenth century did. Now we are worried by circumstances; we want to know exactly what Homer meant when he wrote about the "wine-dark sea" (if "wine-dark sea" be the right translation; I do not know). But if we are historically minded, I think we may perhaps suppose that a time will come when men will be no longer as aware of history as we are. A time will come when men shall care very little about the accidents and circumstances of beauty; they shall care for beauty itself. Perhaps they shall not even care about the names or the biographies of the poets.

This is all to the good, when we think that there are whole nations who think this way. For example, I do not think that in India people have the historical sense. One of the thorns in the flesh of Europeans who write or have written histories of Indian philosophy is that all philosophy is seen as contemporary by the Indians. That is to say, they are interested in the problems themselves, not in the mere biographical fact or historical, chronological fact. That So-and-So was What's-His-Name's master, that he came before, that he wrote under that influence—all those things are nothing to them. They care about the riddle of the universe. I suppose, in a time to come (and I hope this time is around the corner), men will care for beauty, not for the circumstances of beauty. Then we will have translations not only as good (we have them already) but as famous as Chapman's Homer, as Urquhart's Rabelais, as Pope's *Odyssey*.[13] I think this is a consummation devoutly to be wished.

Walter Pater wrote that all art aspires to the condition of music.[1] The obvious reason (I speak as a layman of course) would be that, in music, form and substance cannot be torn asunder. Melody, or any piece of music, is a pattern of sounds and pauses unwinding itself in time, a pattern that I do not suppose can be torn. The melody is merely the pattern, and the emotions it sprang from, and the emotions it awakens. The Austrian critic Hanslick[2] wrote that music is a language that we can use, that we can understand, but that we are unable to translate.

In the case of literature, and especially of poetry, the case is supposed to be quite the opposite. We might tell the plot of *The Scarlet Letter* to a friend of ours who had not read it, and I suppose we could even tell the pattern, the framework, the plot of, say, Yeats's sonnet "Leda and the Swan." So that we fall to thinking of poetry as being a bastard art, as being something of a mongrel.

Robert Louis Stevenson has also spoken of this supposed dual nature of poetry. He says that, in a sense, poetry is nearer to the common man, the man in the street. For the materials of poetry are words, and those words are, he says, the very dialect of life. Words are used for everyday humdrum purposes and are the material of the poet, even as sounds are the material of the musician. Stevenson speaks of words as being mere blocks, mere conveniences. Then he wonders at the poet, who is able to weave those rigid symbols meant for everyday or abstract purposes into a pattern, which he calls "the web."[3] If we accept what Stevenson says, we have a theory of poetry—a theory of words' being made by literature to serve for something beyond their intended use. Words, says Stevenson, are meant for the common everyday commerce of life, and the poet somehow makes of them something magic. I suppose I agree with Stevenson, yet I think he may perhaps be proved wrong. We know that those lonely and admirable Norsemen, in their elegies, were able to convey to us their loneliness, their courage, their loyalty, their feeling for the bleak seas and the bleak wars. Yet I suppose those men who wrote those poems which seem so near to us and come through the centuries—we know that those men would have been hard put to it, had they been made to reason out something in prose. This is the case even with King Alfred. His prose is straightforward; it is efficient for its purposes; but it rings no deep note. He tells us a story—the story may or may not be interesting, but that is all; while there were contemporaries who wrote poetry that still rings, poetry that is still very much living.

Pursuing a historical argument (of course I have taken this example at random; it might be paralleled all over the world), we find that words began not by being abstract, but rather by being concrete—and I suppose "concrete" means much the same thing as "poetic" in this case. Let us consider a word such as "dreary": the word "dreary" meant "bloodstained." Similarly, the word "glad" meant "polished," and the word "threat" meant "a threatening crowd." Those words that now are abstract once had a strong meaning.

We might go on to other examples. Let us take the word "thunder" and look back at the god Thunor, the Saxon counterpart of the Norse Thor. The word *þunor* stood for thunder and for the god; but had we asked the men who came to England with Hengist whether the word stood for the rumbling in the sky or for the angry god, I do not think they would have been subtle enough to understand the difference. I suppose that the word carried both meanings without committing itself very closely to either one of them. I suppose that when they uttered or heard the word "thunder," they at the same time felt the low rumbling in the sky and saw the lightning and thought of the god. The words were packed with magic; they did not have a hard and fast meaning.

Therefore, when speaking of poetry we may say that poetry is not doing what Stevenson thought—poetry is not trying to take a set of logical coins and work them into magic. Rather, it is bringing language back to its original source. Remember that Alfred North Whitehead wrote that, among the many fallacies, there is the fallacy of the perfect dictionary—the fallacy of thinking that for every perception of the senses, for every statement, for every abstract idea, one can find a counterpart, an exact symbol, in the dictionary. And the very fact that languages are different makes us suspect that this does not exist.

For example, in English (or rather in the Scots) we have such words as "eerie" and "uncanny." These words cannot be found in other languages. (Well, of course, we do have the German *unheimlich*.) Why is this so? Because men who spoke other languages had no need for these words—I suppose a nation evolves the words it needs. This observation, made by Chesterton (I think in his book on Watts),[4] amounts to saying that language is not, as we are led to suppose by the dictionary, the invention of academicians or philologists. Rather, it has been evolved through time, through a long time, by peasants, by fishermen, by hunters, by riders. It did not come from the libraries; it came from the fields, from the sea, from rivers, from night, from the dawn.

Thus, we have in language the fact (and this seems obvious to me) that words began, in a sense, as magic. Perhaps there was a moment when the word "light" seemed to be flashing and the word "night" was dark. In the case of "night," we may surmise that it at first stood for the night itself—for its blackness, for its threats, for the shining stars. Then, after ever so long a time, we come to the abstract sense of the word "night"—the period between the twilight of the raven (as the Hebrews had it) and the twilight of the dove, the beginning of day.

Since I have spoken of the Hebrews, we might find an additional example in Jewish mysticism, in the Kabbalah. To the Jews, it seemed obvious there lay a power in words. This is the idea behind all those stories of talismans, of Abracadabras—stories to be found in the *Arabian Nights*. They read in the first chapter of the Torah: "God said, 'Let there be light,' and there was light." So it seemed obvious to them that in the word "light" there lay a strength sufficient to cause light to shine all over the world, a strength sufficient to engender, to beget light. I have done some thinking about this problem of thought and meaning (a problem that of course I will not solve). We spoke earlier about the fact that in music the sound, the form, and the substance cannot be torn asunder—that they are in fact the same thing. And it may be suspected that to a certain degree the same thing happens in poetry.

Let us consider two fragments by two great poets. The first comes from a short piece by the great Irish poet William Butler Yeats: "Bodily decrepitude is wisdom; young / We loved each other and were ignorant."[5] Here we find at the beginning a statement: "Bodily decrepitude is wisdom." This, of course, could be read ironically. Yeats knew quite well that we might attain bodily decrepitude without attaining wisdom. I suppose that wisdom is more important than love; love, than mere happiness. There is something trivial about happiness. We get a statement about happiness in the other part of the stanza. "Bodily decrepitude is wisdom; young / We loved each other and were ignorant."

Now I will take a verse by George Meredith. It runs thus: "Not till the fire is dying in the grate / Look we for any kinship with the stars."[6] This statement, taken at its face value, is false. The idea that we are all interested in philosophy only when we are through with bodily lusts—or when the lusts of the body are through with us—is, I think, false. We know of many passionate young philosophers; think of Berkeley, of Spinoza, and of Schopenhauer. Yet this is quite irrelevant. What is really important is the fact that both fragments—"Bodily decrepitude is wisdom; young / We loved each other and were ignorant," and Meredith's "Not till the fire is dying in the grate / Look we for any kinship with the stars"—taken in the abstract way, mean much the same thing. Yet they strike quite different chords. When we are told—or when I now tell you—that they mean the same thing, you all instinctively and rightly feel that this is irrelevant, that the verses are really different.

I have suspected many a time that meaning is really something added to verse. I know for a fact that we *feel* the beauty of a poem before we even begin to think of a meaning. I do not know whether I have already quoted an example from one of the sonnets of Shakespeare. It runs thus:

> The mortal moon hath her eclipse endured,
> And the sad augurs mock their own presage;
> Incertainties now crown themselves assured,
> And peace proclaims olives of endless age.[7]

Now, if we look at the footnotes, we find that the first two lines—"The mortal moon hath her eclipse endured, / And the sad augurs mock their own presage"—are supposed to be an allusion to Queen Elizabeth—the Virgin Queen, the famous queen compared by the court poets to Diana the chaste, the maiden. I suppose that when Shakespeare wrote these lines, he had both moons in mind. He had that metaphor of "the moon, the Virgin Queen"; and I do not think he could help thinking of the moon in the sky. The point I would like to make is that we do not have to commit ourselves to a meaning—to any one of the meanings. We *feel* the verses before we adopt one, the other, or both of these hypotheses. "The mortal moon hath her eclipse endured, / And the sad augurs mock their own presage" has, at least to me, a beauty far beyond the mere fact of how it is interpreted.

There are, of course, verses that are beautiful and meaningless. Yet they still have a meaning—not to the reason but to the imagination. Let me take a very simple example: "Two red roses across the moon."[8] Here it might be said that the meaning is the image given by the words; but to me, at least, there is no definite image. There is a pleasure in the words, and of course in the lilt of the words, in the music of the words. And let us take another example from William Morris: "'Therefore,' said fair Yoland of the flowers" (fair Yoland is a witch) "'This is the tune of Seven Towers.'"[9] These verses have been torn from their context, and yet I think they stand.

Somehow, though I love English, when I am recalling English verse I find that my language, Spanish, is calling to me. I would like to quote a few lines. If you do not understand them, you may console yourselves by thinking that I do not understand them either, and that they are meaningless. They are beautifully, in a quite lovely way meaningless; they are not meant to mean anything. They come from that too-forgotten Bolivian poet Ricardo Jaimes Freire—a friend of Darío and of Lugones. He wrote them in the last decade of the nineteenth century. I wish I could remember the whole sonnet—I think that something of its sonorous quality would come through to you. But there is no need. I think that these lines should be sufficient. They run thus:

> Peregrina paloma imaginaria
> Que enardeces los últimos amores
> Alma de luz, de música y de flores
> Peregrina paloma imaginaria.[10]

They do not mean anything, they are not meant to mean anything; and yet they stand. They stand as a thing of beauty. They are—at least to me—inexhaustible.

And now, since I have quoted Meredith, I will take another example. This example is different from the others, since it bears a meaning; we feel a conviction that it corresponds to an experience of the poet. And yet, had we to put our finger on that experience, or if the poet were to tell us how he came to these lines, how he attained them, we should be at a loss. The lines are:

> Love, that had robbed us of immortal things,
> This little movement mercifully gave,
> Where I have seen across the twilight wave
> The swan sail with her young beneath her wings.[11]

We find in the first line a reflection that may strike us as strange: "Love, that had robbed us of immortal things"—not (as we might fairly suppose) "love that had made us a gift of immortal things." No—"Love, that had robbed us of immortal things, / This little movement mercifully gave." We are made to feel that he is speaking of himself and of his beloved. "Where I have seen across the twilight wave / The swan sail with her young beneath her wings": here we have the threefold beat of the line—we do not need any anecdotes about the swan, about how she sailed into a river and then into Meredith's poem, and then forever into my memory. We know, or at least *I* know, that I have heard something unforgettable. And I may say of this what Hanslick said of music: I can recall it, I can understand it (not with the mere reason—with a deeper imagination); but I cannot translate it. And I do not think it needs any translation.

Since I have used the word "threefold," I am reminded of a metaphor by a Greek poet of Alexandria. He wrote about "the lyre of the threefold night." This strikes me as being a mighty line. When I looked into the notes, I found that the lyre was Hercules, and that Hercules had been begotten by Jupiter in a night that had the length of three nights, so that the pleasure of the god might be vast. This explanation is quite irrelevant; in fact, perhaps it rather does damage to the verse. It provides us with a small anecdote and takes away something from that wonderful riddle, "the lyre of the threefold night." This should be enough—the riddle. We have no need to read it. The riddle is there.

I have spoken of words standing out at the beginning, when men invented them. I have thought that the word "thunder" might mean not only the sound but the god. And I have spoken of the word "night." When I speak of night, I am inevitably—and happily for us, I think—reminded of the last sentence of the first book in *Finnegans Wake,* wherein Joyce speaks of "the rivering waters of, hitherandthithering waters of. Night!"[12] This is an extreme example of an elaborate style. We feel that such a line could have been written only after centuries of literature. We feel that the line is an invention, a poem—a very complex web, as

Stevenson would have had it. And yet I suspect there was a moment when the word "night" was quite as impressive, was quite as strange, was quite as awe-striking as this beautiful winding sentence: "rivering waters of, hitherandthithering waters of. Night!"

Of course, there are two ways of using poetry—at least, two opposite ways (there are many others, of course). One of the ways of the poet is to use common words and somehow make them uncommon—to evolve magic from them. Quite a good example would be that very English poem, made of understatement, by Edmund Blunden:

> I have been young and now am not too old;
> And I have seen the righteous forsaken,
> His health, his honour and his quality taken.
> This is not what we formerly were told.[13]

Here we have plain words; we have a plain meaning, or at least a plain feeling—and this is more important. But the words do not stand out as they did in that last example from Joyce.

And in this one, which will be mere quotation. It will be three words. They run thus: "Glittergates of elfinbone."[14] "Glittergates" is Joyce's gift to us. And then we have "elfinbone." Of course, when Joyce wrote this, he was thinking of the German for "ivory," *Elfenbein*. *Elfenbein* is a distortion of *Elephantenbein,* "elephant bone." But Joyce saw the possibilities of that word, and he translated it into English; and then we have "elfinbone." I think "elfin" is more beautiful than "elfen." Besides, as we have heard *Elfenbein* so many times, it does not come to us with the shock of surprise, with the shock of amazement, that we find in that new and elegant word "elfinbone."

So we have two ways of writing poetry. People speak generally of a plain style and an elaborate style. I think this is wrong, because what is important, what is all-meaning, is the fact that poetry should be living or dead, not that the style should be plain or elaborate. *That* depends on the poet. We may have, for example, very striking poetry written plainly, and such poetry is, to me, no less admirable—in fact, I sometimes think it is more admirable—than the other. For example, when Stevenson (and as I have disagreed with Stevenson, I want to worship him now) wrote his "Requiem":

> Under the wild and starry sky
> Dig the grave and let me lie
> Glad did I live and gladly die,

And I laid me down with a will.
This be the verse you 'grave for me:
"Here he lies where he longed to be;
Home is the sailor, home from the sea,
And the hunter home from the hill."

This verse is plain language; it is plain and living. But also, the poet must have worked very hard to get it. I do not think that such lines as "Glad did I live and gladly die" come except in those very rare moments when the muse is generous.

I think that our idea of words' being a mere algebra of symbols comes from dictionaries. I do not want to be ungrateful to dictionaries—my favorite reading would be Dr. Johnson, Dr. Skeat, and that composite author, the Shorter Oxford.[15] Yet I think the fact of having long catalogues of words and explanations makes us think that the explanations exhaust the words, and that any one of those coins, of those words, can be exchanged for another. But I think we know—and the poet should feel—that every word stands by itself, that every word is unique. And we get this feeling when a writer uses a little-known word. For example, we think of the word "sedulous" as being a rather far-fetched but interesting word. Yet when Stevenson—I greet him again—wrote that he "played the sedulous ape" to Hazlitt, then suddenly the word comes to life.[16] So this theory (it is not mine, of course—I'm sure it can be found in other authors), this idea of words' beginning as magic and being brought back to magic by poetry, is, I think, a true one.

Now we come to another, quite important question: that of conviction. When we read an author (and we may be thinking of verse, we may be thinking of prose—it is all one), it is essential that we should believe in him. Or rather, that we should attain that "willing suspension of disbelief" of which Coleridge spoke.[17] When I spoke of elaborate verses, of words' standing out, I should have remembered of course:

> Weave a circle round him thrice,
> And close your eyes with holy dread,
> For he on honey-dew hath fed,
> And drunk the milk of Paradise.[18]

Let us now—and this will be our last subject—speak about this conviction that is needed both in prose and in verse. In the case of a novel, for example (and why should we not speak of the novel when we are speaking of poetry?), our conviction lies in the fact that we believe in the central character. If we believe in him, all is well. I am not—and I hope this will not come as a heresy to you—I am not quite sure about the adventures of Don Quixote. I may disbelieve in some of them. I think some of them may be exaggerated. I feel quite sure that when the knight spoke to the squire, he was not weaving those long set speeches. Yet such things are not important; what is really important is the fact that I believe in Don Quixote himself. This is why books such as Azorín's *La ruta de Don Quijote,* or even Unamuno's *Vida de Don Quijote y Sancho,*[19] strike me as somehow irrelevant, for they take the adventures too much in earnest. While I really believe in the knight himself. Even if somebody told me that those things had never happened, I would still go on believing in Don Quixote as I believe in the character of a friend.

I have had the luck to possess many admirable friends, and there are many anecdotes told of them. Some of those anecdotes have—I am sorry to say, I am proud to say—been coined by myself. But they are not false; they are essentially true. De Quincey said that all anecdotes are apocryphal. I think that had he cared to go deeper into the matter, he would have said that they are historically apocryphal but essentially true. If a story is told of a man, then that story resembles him; that story is his symbol. When I think of such dear friends of mine as Don Quixote, Mr. Pickwick, Mr. Sherlock Holmes, Dr. Watson, Huckleberry Finn, Peer Gynt, and so on (I'm not sure I have many more friends), I feel that the men who wrote their histories were drawing the longbow,[20] but that the adventures they evolved were mirrors or adjectives or attributes of those men. That is to say, if we believe in Mr. Sherlock Holmes, then we may look with derision on the hound of the Baskervilles; we need not fear him. So I say that what is important is our believing in a character.

In the case of poetry, there might seem to be a difference—for a writer works with metaphors. The metaphors need not be believed in. What is really important is the fact that we should think they correspond to the writer's emotion. This is, I should say, quite sufficient. For example, when Lugones wrote about the sunset's being "un violento pavo real verde, deliriado en oro,"[21] there is no need to worry about the likeness—or rather the unlikeness—of a sunset to a green peacock. What is important is that we are made to feel that he was stirred by the sunset, that he needed that metaphor to convey his feelings to us. This is what I mean by conviction in poetry.

This has, of course, little to do with plain or elaborate language. When Milton writes, for example (and I am sorry to say, perhaps to reveal to you, that these are the last lines of *Paradise Regained*), "hee unobserv'd / Home to his Mothers house private return'd,"[22] the language is plain enough, but at the same time it is dead. While when he writes "When I consider how my light is spent / Ere half my days, in this dark world,"[23] the language he uses may be elaborate, but it is a living language. In that sense, I think writers like Góngora, John Donne, William Butler Yeats, and James Joyce are justified. Their words, their stanzas may be far-fetched; we may find strange things in them. But we are made to feel that the emotion behind those words is a true one. This should be sufficient for us to tender them our admiration.

I have spoken of several poets today, and I am sorry to say that in the last lecture I shall be speaking of a lesser poet—a poet whose works I never read, but a poet whose works I have to write. I shall speak of myself. And I hope that you will forgive me this quite affectionate anticlimax.

My purpose was to speak about the poet's creed, but, looking into myself, I have found that I have only a faltering kind of creed. This creed may perhaps be useful to me, but hardly to others.

In fact, I think of all poetic theories as being mere tools for the writing of a poem. I suppose there should be as many creeds, as many religions, as there are poets. Though at the end I will say something about my likes and dislikes as to the writing of poetry, I think I will begin with some personal memories, the memories not only of a writer but also of a reader.

I think of myself as being essentially a reader. As you are aware, I have ventured into writing; but I think that what I have read is far more important than what I have written. For one reads what one likes— yet one writes not what one would like to write, but what one is able to write.

My memory carries me back to a certain evening some sixty years ago, to my father's library in Buenos Aires. I see him; I see the gaslight; I could place my hand on the shelves. I know exactly where to find Burton's *Arabian Nights* and Prescott's *Conquest of Peru,* though the library exists no longer. I go back to that already ancient South American evening, and I see my father. I am seeing him at this moment; and I hear his voice saying words that I understood not, but yet I felt. Those words came from Keats, from his "Ode to a Nightingale." I have reread them ever so many times, as you have, but I would like go over them once more. I think this might please my father's ghost, if he is around.

The lines I remember are those that you are recall- ing at this moment:

> Thou wast not born for death, immortal Bird!
> No hungry generations tread thee down;
> The voice I hear this passing night was heard
> In ancient days by emperor and clown:
> Perhaps the self-same song that found a path

A POET'S CREED

Through the sad heart of Ruth, when, sick for home,
She stood in tears amid the alien corn.[1]

I thought I knew all about words, all about language (when one is a child, one feels that one knows many things), but those words came as a revelation to me. Of course, I did not understand them. How could I understand those lines about birds'—about animals'—being somehow eternal, timeless, because they live in the present? We are mortal because we live in the past and in the future—because we remember a time when we did not exist, and foresee a time when we shall be dead. Those verses came to me through their music. I had thought of language as being a way of saying things, of uttering complaints, of saying that one was glad, or sad, and so on. Yet when I heard those lines (and I have been hearing them, in a sense, ever since), I knew that language could also be a music and a passion. And thus was poetry revealed to me.

I have toyed with an idea—the idea that although a man's life is compounded of thousands and thousands of moments and days, those many instants and those many days may be reduced to a single one: the moment when a man knows who he is, when he sees himself face to face. I suppose that when Judas kissed Jesus (if indeed he did so), he felt at that moment that he *was* a traitor, that to be a traitor was his destiny, and that he was being loyal to that evil destiny. We all remember *The Red Badge of Courage,* the story of a man who does not know whether he is a coward or a brave man. Then the moment comes and he knows who he is. When I heard those lines of Keats's, I suddenly felt that that was a great experience. I have been feeling it ever since. And perhaps from that moment (I suppose I may exaggerate for the purposes of a lecture) I thought of myself as being "literary."

That is to say, many things have happened to me, as to all men. I have found joy in many things—in swimming, in writing, in looking at a sunrise or a sunset, in being in love, and so on. But somehow the central fact of my life has been the existence of words and the possibility of weaving those words into poetry. At first, certainly, I was only a reader. Yet I think the happiness of a reader is beyond that of a writer, for a reader need feel no trouble, no anxiety: he is merely out for happiness. And happiness, when you are a reader, is frequent. Thus, before I go on to speak of my literary output, I would like to say a few words about books that have been important to me. I know that this list will abound in omissions, as all lists do. In fact, the danger of making a list is that the omissions stand out and that people think of you as being insensitive.

I spoke a few moments ago about Burton's *Arabian Nights*. When I really think about the *Arabian Nights,* I am thinking not of those many, and ponderous, and pedantic (or rather stilted) volumes, but of what I may call the true *Arabian Nights*—the *Arabian Nights* of Galland and, perhaps, of Edward William Lane.[2] I have done most of my reading in English; most books have come to me through the English language, and I am deeply grateful for that privilege.

When I think of the *Arabian Nights,* the first feeling I have is one of vast freedom. Yet at the same time I know that the book, though vast and free, is limited to a few patterns. For example, the number three occurs in it very frequently. And we have no characters, or rather flat characters (except perhaps for the silent barber). Then we have evil men and good men, rewards and punishments, magic rings and talismans, and so on.

Though we are apt to think of mere size as being somehow brutal, I think there are many books whose essence lies in their being lengthy. For example, in the case of the *Arabian Nights,* we need to think that the book is a large one, that the story goes on, that we may never come to the end of it. We may never have gone through all the thousand and one nights, but the fact that they are there somehow lends wideness to the whole thing. We know that we can delve deeper, that we can roam on, and that the marvels, the magicians, the three beautiful sisters, and so on will always be there, awaiting us.

There are other books I would like to recall— *Huckleberry Finn,* for instance, which was one of the very first I read. I have reread it ever so many times since, and also *Roughing It* (the first days in California), *Life on the Mississippi,* and so on. Had I to analyze *Huckleberry Finn,* I would say that, in order to create a great book, perhaps only one central and very simple fact is needed: there should be something pleasing to the imagination in the very framework of the book. In the case of *Huckleberry Finn,* we feel that the idea of the black man, of the boy, of the raft, of the Mississippi, of the long nights—that these ideas are somehow agreeable to the imagination, are accepted by the imagination.

I would also like to say something about *Don Quixote.* It was one of the first books I ever read through. I remember the very engravings. One knows so little about oneself that, when I read *Don Quixote,* I thought I read it because of the pleasure I found in the archaic style and in the adventures of the knight and the squire. Now I think that my pleasure lay elsewhere—that it came from the character of the knight. I am not sure now that I believe in the adventures, or in the conversations between the knight and the squire; but I know that I believe in the knight's character, and I suppose that the adventures were invented by Cervantes in order to show us the character of the hero.

The same might be said of another book that one may call a minor classic. The same might be said of Mr. Sherlock Holmes and Dr. Watson. I am not sure I believe in the hound of the Baskervilles. I am sure I do not believe in being terrified by a dog painted over with luminous paint. But I am sure that I believe in Mr. Sherlock Holmes and in the strange friendship between him and Dr. Watson.

Of course, one never knows what the future might bring. I suppose the future will bring all things in the long run, and so we may imagine a moment when Don Quixote and Sancho, Sherlock Holmes and Dr. Watson will still exist, though all their adventures may have been blotted out. Yet men, in other languages, may still go on inventing stories to fit those characters—stories that should be as mirrors to the characters. This, for all I know, may happen.

Now I will jump over the years and go to Geneva. I was then a very unhappy young man. I suppose young men are fond of unhappiness; they do their best to be unhappy, and they generally achieve it. Then I discovered an author who doubtless was a very happy man. It must have been in 1916 that I came to Walt Whitman, and then I felt ashamed of my unhappiness. I felt ashamed, for I had tried to be still more unhappy by reading Dostoevsky. Now that I have reread Walt Whitman, and also biographies of him, I suppose that perhaps when Walt Whitman read his *Leaves of Grass* he may have said to himself: "Oh! if only I were Walt Whitman, a kosmos, of Manhattan the son!"[3] Because doubtless he was a very different kind of man. Doubtless he evolved "Walt Whitman" from himself—a kind of fantastic projection.

At the same time, I also discovered a very different writer. I also discovered—and I was also overwhelmed by—Thomas Carlyle. I read *Sartor Resartus,* and I can recall many of its pages; I know them by heart. Carlyle sent me to the study of German. I remember I bought Heine's *Lyrisches Intermezzo* and a German-English dictionary. After a while, I found I could dispense with the dictionary and could go on reading about his nightingales, his moons, his pine trees, his love, and so on.

But what I really wanted and did not find at the time was the idea of Germanism. The idea, I suppose, was evolved not by the Germanic people themselves but by a Roman gentleman, Tacitus. I was led by Carlyle to think that I could find it in German literature. I found many other things; I am very grateful to Carlyle for having sent me to Schopenhauer, to Hölderlin, to Lessing, and so on. But the idea I had—the idea of men not at all intellectual but given over to loyalty, to bravery, to a manly submission to fate—this I did not find, for example, in the *Nibelungenlied*. All of that seemed too romantic for me. I was to find it years and years afterwards in the Norse sagas and in the study of Old English poetry.

There I found at last what I had been looking for when I was a young man. In Old English I discovered a harsh language, but a language whose harshness made for a certain kind of beauty and also for very deep feeling (even if, perhaps, not very deep thinking). In poetry, feeling is enough, I suppose. If the feeling comes through to you, it should be sufficient. I was led to the study of Old English by my inclination to the metaphor. I had read in Lugones that the metaphor was the essential element of literature, and I accepted that dictum. Lugones wrote that all words were originally metaphors. This is true, but it is also true that in order to understand most words, you have to forget about the fact of their being metaphors. For example, if I say, "Style should be plain," then I don't think we should remember that "style" *(stylus)* meant "pen," and that "plain" means "flat," because in that case we would never understand it.

Allow me to go back again to my boyhood days and remember other authors who struck me. I wonder if it has been often remarked that Poe and Oscar Wilde are really writers for boys. At least, the stories of Poe impressed me when I was a boy, yet now I can hardly reread them without feeling rather uncomfortable over the style of the author. In fact, I can quite understand what Emerson meant when he called Edgar Allan Poe the "jingle" man. I suppose that this fact of being a writer for boys might be applied to many other writers. In some cases, such a description is unjust—in the case of Stevenson, for example, or of Kipling; for although they write for boys, they also write for men. But there are other writers whom one must read when one is young, because if one comes to

them when one is old and gray and full of days, then
the reading of those writers can hardly be pleasant. It
may be blasphemy to say that in order to enjoy
Baudelaire and Poe we should be young. Afterwards
it is difficult. One has to put up with so many things;
one has to think of history, and so on.

As to the metaphor, I should add that I now
see that metaphor is a far more complicated thing
than I thought. It is not merely a comparing of one
thing to another—saying, "the moon is like . . . ," and
so on. No—it may be done in a more subtle way.
Think of Robert Frost. You of course remember the
lines:

> For I have promises to keep
> And miles to go before I sleep
> And miles to go before I sleep.

If we take the last two lines, the first—"And miles to
go before I sleep"—is a statement: the poet is thinking of miles and of sleep. But when he repeats it,
"And miles to go before I sleep," the line becomes a
metaphor; for "miles," stands for "days," for "years,"
for a long stretch of time, while "sleep" presumably
stands for "death." Perhaps I am doing no good for
us by pointing this out. Perhaps the pleasure lies not

A POET'S CREED

in our translating "miles" into "years" and "sleep" into "death," but rather in feeling the implication.

The same thing might be said of that other very fine poem of his, "Acquainted with the Night." In the beginning, "I have been one acquainted with the night" may mean literally what he is telling us. But the line comes again at the end:

> O luminary clock against the sky,
> Proclaimed the time was neither wrong nor right.
> I have been one acquainted with the night.

Then we are made to think of the night as an image of evil—of sexual evil, I suppose.

I spoke a moment ago about Don Quixote, and about Sherlock Holmes; I said that I could believe in the characters but not in their adventures, and hardly in the words that the authors put in their mouths. Now we wonder whether we could find a book where the exact contrary occurred. Could we find a book in whose characters we disbelieved but where we might believe the story? Here I remember another book that struck me: I remember Melville's *Moby-Dick*. I am not sure if I believe in Captain Ahab, I am not sure that I believe in his feud with the white whale; I can hardly tell the characters apart. Yet I believe in the story—that is, I believe in it as in a kind of parable (though I don't exactly know what it's a parable of—perhaps a parable of the struggle against evil, of the wrong way of fighting evil). I wonder if there are any books of which this might be said. In *The Pilgrim's Progress,* I think I believe both in the allegory and in the characters. This should be looked into.

Remember that the Gnostics said the only way to be rid of a sin is to commit it, because afterwards you repent it. In regard to literature, they were essentially right. If I have attained the happiness of writing four or five tolerable pages, after writing fifteen intolerable volumes, I have come to that feat not only through many years but also through the method of trial and error. I think I have committed not all the possible mistakes—because mistakes are innumerable—but many of them.

For example, I began, as most young men do, by thinking that free verse is easier than the regular forms of verse. Today I am quite sure that free verse is far more difficult than the regular and classic forms. The proof—if proof be needed—is that literature begins with verse. I suppose the explanation would be that once a pattern is evolved—a pattern of rhymes, of assonances, of alliterations, of long and short syllables, and so on—you only have to repeat the pattern. While, if you attempt prose (and prose, of course, comes long after verse), then you need, as Stevenson pointed out, a more subtle pattern. Because the ear is led to expect something, and then it does not get what it expects. Something else is given to it; and that something else should be, in a sense, a failure and also a satisfaction. So that unless you take the precaution of being Walt Whitman or Carl Sandburg, then free verse is more difficult. At least I have found, now when I am near my journey's end, that the classic forms of verse are easier. Another facility, another easiness, may lie in the fact that once you have written a certain line, once you have resigned yourself to a certain line, then you have committed yourself to a certain rhyme. And since rhymes are not infinite, your work is made easier for you.

Of course, what is important is what is behind the verse. I began by trying—as all young men do—to disguise myself. At first, I was so mistaken that at the time I read Carlyle and Whitman, I thought that Carlyle's way of writing prose was the only possible one, and that Whitman's way of writing verse was the only possible one. I made no attempt whatever to reconcile the very strange fact that two opposite men had attained the perfection of prose and of verse.

When I began writing, I always said to myself that my ideas were very shallow—that if a reader saw through them, he would despise me. And so I disguised myself. In the beginning, I tried to be a seventeenth-century Spanish writer with a certain knowledge of Latin. My knowledge of Latin was quite slight. I do not think of myself now as a seventeenth-century Spanish writer, and my attempts to be Sir Thomas Browne in Spanish failed utterly. Or perhaps they evolved quite a dozen fine-sounding lines. Of course, I was out for purple patches. Now I think that purple patches are a mistake. I think they are a mistake because they are a sign of vanity, and the reader thinks of them as being signs of vanity. If the reader thinks that you have moral defect, there is no reason whatever why he should admire you or put up with you.

Then I fell into a very common mistake: I did my best to be—of all things—modern. There is a character in Goethe's *Wilhelm Meisters Lehrjahre* who says: "Well, you may say of me what you like, but nobody will deny that I am a contemporary." I see no difference between that quite absurd character in Goethe's novel and the wish to be modern. Because we *are* modern; we don't have to strive to be modern. It is not a case of subject matter or of style.

If you look into Sir Walter Scott's *Ivanhoe* or (to take a very different example) into Flaubert's *Salammbô*, you may tell the date when those books were written. Though Flaubert spoke of *Salammbô* as a *"roman cartaginois,"* any reader worth his salt will know after reading the first page that the book was not written in Carthage, but was written by a very intelligent Frenchman of the nineteenth century. As for *Ivanhoe*, we are not taken in by the castles and the knights and the Saxon swineherds and so on. All the time, we know that we are reading an eighteenth- or nineteenth-century author.

Besides, we are modern by the very simple fact that we live in the present. Nobody has yet discovered the art of living in the past, and not even the futurists have discovered the secret of living in the future. We are modern whether we want to be or not. Perhaps the very fact of my attacking modernity now is a way of being modern.

When I began writing stories, I did my best to trick them out. I labored over the style, and sometimes those stories were hidden under the many over-layings. For example, I thought of a quite good plot; then I wrote the story "El inmortal."[4] The idea behind that story—and the idea might come as a surprise to any of you who have read the story—is that if a man were immortal, then in the long run (and the run *would* be long, of course), he would have said all things, done all things, written all things. I took as my example Homer; I thought of him (if indeed he existed) as having written his *Iliad*. Then Homer would go on living, and he would change as the generations of men have changed. Eventually, of course, he would forget his Greek, and in due time he would forget that he had been Homer. A moment may come when we will think of Pope's translation of Homer as being not only a fine work of art (indeed it is), but as being true to the original. This idea of Homer forgetting that he was Homer is hidden under the many structures I wove around the book. In fact, when I reread that story a couple of years ago, I found it a weariness of the flesh, and I had to go back to my old plan to see that the story would have been quite good had I been content to write it down simply and not permit so many purple patches and so many strange adjectives and metaphors.

I think I have come not to a certain wisdom but perhaps to a certain sense. I think of myself as a writer. What does being a writer mean to me? It means simply being true to my imagination. When I write something, I think of it not as being factually true (mere fact is a web of circumstances and accidents), but as being true to something deeper. When I write a story, I write it because somehow I believe in it—not as one believes in mere history, but rather as one believes in a dream or in an idea.

I think perhaps we may be led astray by one of the studies I value most: the study of the history of literature. I wonder (and I hope this is not blasphemy) if we are not too aware of history. Being aware of the history of literature—or of any other art, for that matter—is really a form of unbelieving, a form of skepticism. If I say to myself, for example, that Wordsworth and Verlaine were very good nineteenth-century poets, then I may fall into the danger of thinking that time has somehow destroyed them, that they are not as good now as they were. I think the ancient idea—that we might allow perfection to art without taking into account the dates—was a braver one.

I have read several histories of Indian philosophy. The authors (Englishmen, Germans, Frenchmen, Americans, and so on) always wonder at the fact that in India people have no historical sense—that they treat all thinkers as if they were contemporary. They translate the words of ancient philosophy into the modern jargon of today's philosophy. But this stands for something brave. This stands for the idea that one *believes* in philosophy or that one *believes* in poetry—that things beautiful once can go on being beautiful still.

Though I suppose I am being quite unhistorical when I say this (since of course the meanings and connotations of words are changing), still I think there are lines—for example, when Virgil wrote "Ibant obscuri sola sub nocte per umbram"[5] (I wonder if I am scanning this as I should—my Latin is very rusty), or when an old English poet wrote "Norþan sniwde . . . ,"[6] or when we read "Music to hear, why hear'st thou music sadly? / Sweets with sweets war not, joy delights in joy"[7]—where somehow we are beyond time. I think that there is an eternity in beauty; and this, of course, is what Keats had in mind when he wrote "A thing of beauty is a joy forever."[8] We accept this verse, but we accept it as a kind of right, as a kind of formula. Sometimes I am courageous and hopeful enough to think that it may be true—that though all men write in time, are involved in circumstances and accidents and failures of time, somehow things of eternal beauty may be achieved.

When I write, I try to be loyal to the dream and not to the circumstances. Of course, in my stories (people tell me I should speak about them) there are true circumstances, but somehow I have felt that those circumstances should always be told with a certain amount of untruth. There is no satisfaction in telling a story as it actually happened. We have to change things, even if we think them insignificant; if we don't, we should think of ourselves not as artists but perhaps as mere journalists or historians. Though I suppose all true historians have known that they can be quite as imaginative as novelists. For example, when we read Gibbon, the pleasure we get from him is quite akin to the pleasure we get from reading a great novelist. After all, he knew very little about his characters. I suppose he had to imagine the circumstances. He must have thought of himself as having created, in a sense, the decline and fall of the Roman Empire. And he did it so wonderfully that I do not care to accept any other explanation.

Had I to give advice to writers (and I do not think they need it, because everyone has to find out things for himself), I would tell them simply this: I would ask them to tamper as little as they can with their own work. I do not think tinkering does any good. The moment comes when one has found out what one can do—when one has found one's natural voice, one's rhythm. Then I do not think that slight emendations should prove useful.

When I write, I do not think of the reader (because the reader is an imaginary character), and I do not think of myself (perhaps *I* am an imaginary character also), but I think of what I am trying to convey and I do my best not to spoil it. When I was young, I believed in expression. I had read Croce, and the reading of Croce did me no good. I wanted to express everything. I thought, for example, that if I needed a sunset I should find the exact word for a sunset—or rather, the most surprising metaphor. Now I have come to the conclusion (and this conclusion may sound sad) that I no longer believe in expression: I believe only in allusion. After all, what are words? Words are symbols for shared memories. If I use a word, then you should have some experience of what the word stands for. If not, the word means nothing to you. I think we can only allude, we can only try to make the reader imagine. The reader, if he is quick enough, can be satisfied with our merely hinting at something.

This makes for efficiency—and in my own case it also makes for laziness. I have been asked why I have never attempted a novel. Laziness, of course, is the first explanation. But there is another one. I have never read any novel without feeling a certain weariness. Novels include padding; I think padding may be an essential part of the novel, for all I know. Yet I have read many short stories over and over again. I find that in a short story by, for example, Henry James or Rudyard Kipling you get quite as much complexity, and in a more pleasurable way, as you may get out of a long novel.

I think that this is what my creed comes to. When I promised "a poet's creed," I thought, very credulously, that once I had given five lectures I would, in the process, have evolved a creed of some kind. But I think I owe it to you to say that I have no particular creed, except those few precautions and misgivings I have been talking to you about.

When I am writing something, I try not to understand it. I do not think intelligence has much to do with the work of a writer. I think that one of the sins of modern literature is that it is too self-conscious. For example, I think of French literature as being one of the great literatures in the world (I don't suppose anybody could doubt this). Yet I have been made to feel that French authors are generally too self-conscious. A French writer begins by defining himself before he quite knows what he is going to write. He says:

What should (for example) a Catholic born in such-and-such province, and being a bit of a socialist, write? Or: How should we write after the Second World War? I suppose there are many people all over the world who labor under those illusory problems.

When I write (of course, I may not be a fair example, but merely an awful warning), I try to forget all about myself. I forget about my personal circumstances. I do not try, as I tried once, to be a "South American writer." I merely try to convey what the dream is. And if the dream be a dim one (in my case, it usually is), I do not try to beautify it, or even to understand it. Maybe I have done well, for every time I read an article about me—and somehow there seem to be quite a lot of people doing that sort of thing—I am generally amazed and very grateful for the deep meanings that have been read into those quite haphazard jottings of mine. Of course, I am grateful to them, for I think of writing as being a kind of collaboration. That is to say, the reader does his part of the work; he is enriching the book. And the same thing happens when one is lecturing.

You may think now and then that you have heard a good lecture. In that case, I must congratulate you, because, after all, you have been working with me. Had it not been for you, I don't think the lectures would have seemed particularly good, or even tolerable. I hope that you have been collaborating with me tonight. And since this night is different from other nights, I would like to say something about myself.

I came to America six months ago. In my country I am practically (to repeat the title of a famous book by Wells) the Invisible Man.[9] Here, I am somehow visible. Here, people have read me—they have read me so much that they cross-examine me on stories I have forgotten all about. They ask me why So-and-So was silent before he answered, and I wonder who So-and-So was, why he was silent, what he answered. I hesitate to tell them the truth. I say that So-and-So was silent before he answered because generally one is silent before one answers. And yet, all these things have made me happy. I think you are quite mistaken if you admire (I wonder if you do) my writing. But I think of it as a very generous mistake. I think that one should try to believe in things even if they let you down afterwards.

If I am joking now, I do so because I feel something within me. I am joking because I really feel what this means to me. I know that I shall look back on this night. I will wonder: Why did not I say what I should have said? Why did not I say what these months in

America have meant to me—what all these unknown and known friends have meant to me? But I suppose that somehow my feeling is coming through to you.

I have been asked to say some verses of mine; so I will go over a sonnet, the sonnet on Spinoza. The fact that many of you may have no Spanish will make it a finer sonnet. As I have said, meaning is not important—what is important is a certain music, a certain way of saying things. Maybe, though the music may not be there, you will feel it. Or rather, since I know you are very kind, you will invent it for me.

Now we come to the sonnet, "Spinoza":

> Las traslúcidas manos del judío
> Labran en la penumbra los cristales
> Y la tarde que muere es miedo y frío.
> (Las tardes a las tardes son iguales.)
> Las manos y el espacio de jacinto
> Que palidece en el confín del Ghetto
> Casi no existen para el hombre quieto
> Que está soñando un claro laberinto.
> No lo turba la fama, ese reflejo
> De sueños en el sueño de otro espejo
> Y el temeroso amor de las doncellas.
> Libre de la metáfora y del mito,
> Labra un arduo o cristal: el infinito
> Mapa de Aquél que es todas Sus estrellas.[10]

A POET'S CREED

NOTES

"OF THIS AND THAT VERSATILE CRAFT"

INDEX

NOTES

Unless otherwise stated, all translations used in this book are by the editor.

1. The Riddle of Poetry

1. William Shakespeare, Sonnet 86.

2. Borges is no doubt thinking of Plato's *Phaedrus* (section 275d), where Socrates says: "I cannot help feeling, Phaedrus, that writing is unfortunately like painting; for the creations of the painter have the attitude of life, and yet if you ask them a question they preserve a solemn silence" (trans. Benjamin Jowett). According to Socrates, things should be taught and communicated orally; this is "the true way of writing" (278b). To write with pen and ink is to write "in water," since the words cannot defend themselves. The spoken word—"the living word of knowledge, which has a soul"—is thus superior to the written word, which is nothing more than its image. The words written with pen and ink are as defenseless as those who trust them.

3. Rafael Cansinos-Asséns is the Andalusian writer of whose "magnificent memories" Borges never tired of speaking. While in Madrid in the early 1920s, the young Argentine frequented his literary circle *(tertulia)*. "Meeting him, I seemed to encounter the libraries of the Orient and of the West" (Roberto Alifano, *Conversaciones con Borges* [Buenos Aires: Debate, 1986], 101–102). Cansinos-Asséns, who boasted that he could salute the stars in fourteen languages (or seventeen, as Borges says on another occasion)—both classical and modern—did translations from French, Arabic, Latin, and Hebrew. See Jorge Luis Borges and Oswaldo Ferrari, *Diálogos* (Barcelona: Seix Barral, 1992), 37.

4. Macedonio Fernández (1874–1952) was a proponent of absolute idealism who exerted a steady fascination upon Borges. He was one of the two authors whom Borges compared to Adam for their sense of a beginning (the other was Whitman). This most unconventional Argentine declared, "I write only because writing helps me think." He produced a large number of poems (collected in *Poesías completas,* ed. Carmen de Mora [Madrid: Visor, 1991]) and a great deal of prose, including *Una novela que comienza* (A Novel That Begins), *Papelas de recienvenido: Continuación de la nada* (Papers of the Recently Arrived: A Continuation of Nothing), *Museo de la novela de la eterna: Primera novela buena* (Museum of the Novel of the Eternal: The First Good Novel), *Manera de una psique sin cuerpo* (Manner of a Bodiless Psyche), and *Adriana Buenos Aires: Última novela mala* (Adriana Buenos Aires: The Last Bad

Novel). Borges and Fernández cofounded the literary journal *Proa* in 1922.

5. Shakespeare, *Hamlet,* Act 3, scene 1, lines 57–90.

6. Dante Gabriel Rossetti, "Inclusiveness," Sonnet 29, in Rossetti, *Poems,* 1st ed. (London: Ellis, 1870), 217.

7. Heraclitus, Fragment 41, in *The Fragments of the Work of Heraclitus of Ephesus on Nature,* trans. Ingram Bywater (Baltimore: N. Murray, 1889). See also Plato, *Cratylus,* 402a; and Aristotle, *Metaphysics,* 101a, n3.

8. Robert Browning (1812–1889), "Bishop Blougram's Apology," lines 182–184.

9. Borges' poem "To Rafael Cansinos-Asséns" runs thus:

> Long and final passage over the breathtaking height of the
>   trestle's span.
> At our feet the wind gropes for sails and the stars throb in-
>   tensely.
> We relish the taste of the night, transfixed by
> darkness-night become now, again, a habit of our flesh.
> The final night of our talking before the sea-miles part us.
> Still ours is the silence
> where, like meadows, the voices glitter.
> Dawn is still a bird lost in the most distant vileness of the
>   world.
> This last night of all, sheltered from the great wind of ab-
>   sence.
> The inwardness of Good-bye is tragic,
> like that of every event in which Time is manifest.
> It is bitter to realize that we shall not even have the stars in
>   common.

When evening is quietness in my patio,
from your pages morning will rise.
Your winter will be the shadow of my summer,
and your light the glory of my shadow.
Still we persist together.
Still our two voices achieve understanding
like the intensity and tenderness of sundown.

Translated by Robert Fitzgerald, in Jorge Luis Borges, *Se-lected Poems, 1923–1967,* ed. Norman Thomas di Giovanni (New York: Delacorte, 1972), 193, 248.

10. *The Seafarer,* ed. Ida Gordon (Manchester: Man-chester University Press, 1979), 37, lines 31b–33a. Borges' translation "rime bound the fields" avoids the repetition of "earth" present in the original. A literal translation would be: "rime bound the earth."

11. This famous quotation ("Quid est ergo tempus? Si nemo ex me quaerat scio; si quaerenti explicare velim, nescio") is from Augustine's *Confessions,* 11.14.

2. The Metaphor

1. Leopoldo Lugones (1874–1938), a major Argentine writer of the early twentieth century, was initially a modern-ist. His *Lunario sentimental* (Sentimental Moonery) (Bue-nos Aires: Moen, 1909) is an eclectic volume of poetry, short stories, and plays that revolve around the theme of the moon; it caused a scandal when it came out, both for break-ing with the already established highbrow *modernismo* and for mocking the audiences of this trend. Lugones is often

quoted and commented on in Borges' works. See, for example, Borges, "Leopoldo Lugones, *El imperio jesuítico,*" *Biblioteca personal,* in *Obras completas,* vol. 4 (Buenos Aires: Emecé Editores, 1996), 461–462, where Lugones is described as "a man of elemental convictions and passions."

2. Borges is referring to *An Etymological Dictionary of the English Language,* by the Reverend Walter W. Skeat, which was first published in Oxford, England, 1879–1882.

3. What we know today as the Greek Anthology consists of about 4,500 short poems by some 300 authors, representing Greek literature from the seventh century B.C. to the tenth century A.D. These are preserved mainly in two overlapping collections, the Palatine Anthology (which was compiled in the tenth century and takes its name from the Palatine Library in Heidelberg) and the Planudean Anthology (which dates from the fourteenth century and is named for the rhetorician and compiler Maximus Planudes). The Planudean Anthology was first printed in Florence in 1484; the Palatine Anthology was rediscovered in 1606.

4. G. K. Chesterton (1874–1936), "A Second Childhood," in *The Collected Poems of G. K. Chesterton* (London: Cecil Palmer, 1927), 70 (stanza 5).

5. Andrew Lang, *Alfred Tennyson,* 2nd ed. (Edinburgh: Blackwood, 1901), 17. Lang actually says that the line is from Tennyson's poem "The Mystic," published in 1830.

6. *Of Time and the River,* by Thomas Wolfe, was first published in 1935.

7. Heraclitus, Fragment 41, in *The Fragments of the*

Work of Heraclitus of Ephesus on Nature, trans. Ingram Bywater (Baltimore: N. Murray, 1889). See also Plato, *Cratylus,* 402a; and Aristotle, *Metaphysics,* 1010a, n3.

8. Jorge Manrique (1440–1479), "Coplas de Don Jorge Manrique por la muerte de su padre," stanza 3, lines 25–30. For a reprint, see Manrique, *Poesía,* ed. Jesús-Manuel Alda Tesán, 13th ed. (Madrid: Cátedra, 1989).

9. Longfellow's translation runs:

> Our lives are rivers, gliding free
> To that unfathomed, boundless sea,
> The silent grave!
> Thither all earthly pomp and boast
> Roll, to be swallowed up and lost
> In one dark wave.

10. Shakespeare, *The Tempest,* Act 4, scene 1, lines 156–158: "We are such stuff / As dreams are made on, and our little life / Is rounded with a sleep."

11. Walther von der Vogelweide was a German medieval poet (c.1170–c.1230), one of the twelve "apostles" of the bards *(zwöllf Schirmherrenden Meistersängers).* The first three lines of his poem "Die Elegie" (The Elegy) read:

> Owêr sint verswunden
> ist mir mîn leben getroumet,
> daz ich ie wânde ez wære.

In Walther von der Vogelweide, *Gedichte: Mittelhochdeutscher Text und Übertragung,* ed. Peter Wapnewski

(Frankfurt: Fischer, 1982), 108. Borges' version of the quote is half in Middle High German, half in modern German.

12. There is no reference to "iron sleep" among the ninety-one occurrences of "sleep" listed in a concordance to Homer. Borges may be thinking of Virgil's *Aeneid*, in John Dryden's translation: "Dire dreams to thee, and iron sleep, he bears" (Book 5, line 1095); "An iron sleep his stupid eyes oppress'd" (Book 12, line 467).

13. Robert Frost, "Stopping by Woods on a Snowy Evening," stanza 4, lines 13–16.

14. Among other achievements, León Dujovne translated the *Sepher Ietzirah* from Hebrew into Spanish.

15. See *"Beowulf" and the Finnesburg Fragment*, translated into modern English by John R. Clark Hall (London: Allen and Unwin, 1958).

16. From Poem 51 of E. E. Cummings' collection *W (ViVa)*, published in 1931 (when Cummings was thirty-seven). Borges quotes the first four lines of the third stanza.

17. Farid al-Din Attar (died ca. 1230) was the author of *Mantiq al-tayr*, in English *The Conference of the Birds*, trans. Afkham Darbandi and Dick Davis (Harmondsworth: Penguin, 1984). Omar Khayyám (fl. eleventh century) was the author of the *Rubáiyát*, translated in 1859 by Edward FitzGerald, whose version subsequently went through many editions. Hafiz of Shiraz (died 1389–1390) was the author of *Divan*, translated from the Persian by Gertrude Lowthian Bell (London: Octagon Press, 1979).

18. Rudyard Kipling, *From Sea to Sea* (Garden City, N.Y.:

Doubleday Page, 1912), 386. The quote is from Dean Burgon's poem "Petra" (1845), which echoes Samuel Rogers' "Italy: A Farewell" (1828): "many a temple half as old as Time."

19. Shakespeare, Sonnet 2.

20. A *kenning* (plural *kenningar)* is a multi-noun paraphrase used in place of a single noun. *Kenningar* are common in Old Germanic verse, especially in skaldic poetry, and to a lesser extent in Eddic literature. Borges discussed such phrases in his essay "Las *kenningar,"* part of *La historia de la eternidad* (The History of Eternity; 1936), and in *Literaturas germánicas medievales* (Germanic Medieval Literatures; 1951), written with María Esther Vázquez.

21. This is the first line of Byron's eighteen-line poem "She Walks in Beauty, Like the Night," first published in his collection *Hebrew Melodies* (1815), a series of songs to be set to adaptations of traditional Jewish tunes by the musician Isaac Nathan.

3. The Telling of the Tale

1. William Wordsworth, "With Ships the Sea Was Sprinkled Far and Nigh," collected in his volume *Poems,* 1815.

2. William Shakespeare, Sonnet 8.

3. Homer, *The Iliad: The Story of Achillês,* trans. William H. D. Rouse (New York: New American Library, 1964).

4. See Borges, "Las *kenningar,"* in *La historia de la eternidad* (Buenos Aires: Emecé Editores, 1936), which deals extensively with Snorri Sturluson (1179–1241), the Ice-

landic master of the Edda. Borges' poem dedicated to him runs thus:

> You, who bequeathed a mythology
> Of ice and fire to filial recall,
> Who chronicled the violent glory
> Of your defiant Germanic stock,
> Discovered in amazement one night
> Of swords that your untrustworthy flesh
> Trembled. On that night without sequel
> You realized you were a coward. . . .
> In the darkness of Iceland the salt
> Wind moves the mounting sea. Your house is
> Surrounded. You have drunk to the dregs
> Unforgettable dishonor. On
> Your head, your sickly face, falls the sword,
> As it fell so often in your book.

Translated by Richard Howard and César Rennert, in Jorge Luis Borges, *Selected Poems, 1923–1967* (bilingual edition), ed. Norman Thomas di Giovanni (New York: Delacorte, 1972), 163.

5. See Samuel Butler (1835–1902), *The Authoress of the "Odyssey," Where and When She Wrote, Who She Was, the Use She Made of the "Iliad," and How the Poem Grew under Her Hands,* ed. David Grene (Chicago: University of Chicago Press, 1967).

6. Shakespeare, *King Henry the Fourth, Part I*, Act 1, scene 1, lines 25–27: "those blessed feet / Which fourteen hundred years ago were nail'd / For our advantage on the bitter cross."

7. William Langland (1330?–1400?), *The Vision of Piers the Plowman,* ed. Kate M. Warren (London: T. Fisher Unwin, 1895).

8. Henry James, *The Aspern Papers* (London: Martin Secker, 1919).

9. *Völsunga Saga: The Story of the Volsungs and Niblungs,* ed. H. Halliday Sparling, translated from the Icelandic by Eiríkr Magnússon and William Morris (London: W. Scott, 1870).

10. T. E. Lawrence, *Seven Pillars of Wisdom: A Triumph* (London: J. Cape, 1935).

11. Henri Barbusse, *Le Feu: Journal d'une escouade* (Paris: Flammarion, 1915).

12. G. K. Chesterton, "The Ballad of the White Horse" (1911), in *The Collected Poems of G. K. Chesterton* (London: Cecil Palmer, 1927), 225. This is a long poem of some 530 stanzas. Borges quotes from Book 3, stanza 22.

4. Word-Music and Translation

1. That prose translation was published in the *Contemporary Review* (London), November 1876.

2. Tennyson, "The Battle of Brunanburh," in *The Complete Poetical Works of Tennyson* (Boston: Houghton Mifflin, 1898), 485 (stanza 3, lines 6–7).

3. This is the first of the eight stanzas of San Juan's "Noche oscura del alma," or, as the Golden Age Castilian has it, "Canciones de el alma que se goza de aver llegado al alto estado de la perfectión, que es la unión con Dios, por

el camino de la negación espiritual." E. Allison Peers translates it as:

> Upon a darksome night,
> Kindling with love in flame of yearning keen
> —O moment of delight!—
> I went by all unseen,
> New-hush'd to rest in the house where I had been.

Saint John of the Cross (1542–1591), *The Spiritual Canticle and Poems*, trans. E. Allison Peers (London: Burns and Oates, 1935), 441. Willis Barnstone's translation runs:

> On a black night,
> starving for love and dark in flames,
> Oh lucky turn and flight!
> unseen I slipped away,
> my house at last was calm and safe.

Saint John of the Cross, *The Poems of Saint John of the Cross,* trans. Willis Barnstone (New York: New Directions, 1972), 39.

4. Symons translated it as "The Obscure Night of the Soul." See William Butler Yeats, ed., *The Oxford Book of Modern Verse, 1892–1935* (New York: Oxford University Press, 1936), 77–78.

5. Roy Campbell, *Collected Poems* (London: Bodley Head, 1949; rpt. 1955), 164–165. Campbell takes the first phrase of the Spanish original as the title of his translation: "En una noche oscura."

6. The phrase "grand translateur" comes from a *ballade* by Eustache Deschamps, Chaucer's French contemporary. The refrain is: "et translateur, noble Geoffroy Chaucier."

7. This is the first line of Chaucer's "Parlement of Fowles."

8. Tennyson, "The Battle of Brunanburh," in *The Complete Poetical Works,* 486 (stanza 13, lines 4–5).

9. According to tradition, Hengist and Horsa were brothers who led the Jutish invasion of Britain in the mid-fifth century and founded the kingdom of Kent.

10. Francis William Newman (1805–1897) not only was a classical scholar and translator, but wrote extensively on religion, politics, philosophy, economics, morality, and other social issues. His translation of the *Iliad* was published in 1856 (London: Walton and Maberly).

11. Omar Khayyám (1048?–1122), *Rubáiyát,* trans. Edward FitzGerald (1809–1883), ed. Carl J. Weber (Waterville, Maine: Colby College Press, 1959). FitzGerald's version was first published in London in 1859.

12. The line is from Horace, *Ars poetica,* 359: "Indignor quandoque bonus dormitat Homerus" ("I'm aggrieved when sometimes even excellent Homer nods").

13. George Chapman's translation of the *Iliad* was published in 1614; his *Odyssey,* in 1614–1615. Thomas Urquhart (or Urchard) published his translation of the five volumes of Rabelais between 1653 and 1694. Alexander Pope's translation of the *Odyssey* appeared in 1725–1726.

5. Thought and Poetry

1. "All art constantly aspires towards the condition of music." Walter Pater, "The School of Giorgione," in Pater, *Studies in the History of the Renaissance* (1873).

2. Eduard Hanslick (1825–1904), Austrian music critic, was the author of *Vom Musikalisch-Schönen,* first published in 1854. In English: *The Beautiful in Music,* trans. Gustav Cohen (London: Novello, 1891).

3. See Stevenson's essay "On Some Technical Elements of Style in Literature" (section 2, "The Web"), in Robert Louis Stevenson, *Essays of Travel and in the Art of Writing* (New York: Charles Scribner's Sons, 1923), 253–277, esp. 256 and 259: "The motive and end of any art whatever is to make a pattern.... The web, then, or the pattern: a web at once sensuous and logical, an elegant and pregnant texture: that is style, that is the foundation of the art of literature."

4. G. K. Chesterton, *G. F. Watts* (London: Duckworth, 1904). Borges may be thinking of pp. 91–94, where Chesterton discusses signs, symbols, and the mutability of language.

5. William Butler Yeats, "After Long Silence," in W. B. Yeats, *The Poems,* ed. Richard J. Finneran (New York: Macmillan, 1983), 265 (lines 7–8).

6. George Meredith, *Modern Love* (1862), Sonnet 4.

7. Shakespeare, Sonnet 107.

8. William Morris, "Two Red Roses across the Moon," in Morris, *"The Defence of Guenevere" and Other Poems* (London: Longmans, Green, 1896), 223–225. This line is the refrain to each of the nine stanzas.

9. William Morris, "The Tune of Seven Towers," in *"The Defence of Guenevere" and Other Poems,* 199–201. Again, Borges quotes the refrain. The poem was written in 1858, and was inspired by Dante Gabriel Rossetti's painting *The Tune of Seven Towers* (1857).

10. The lines could be translated as follows:

> Wandering imaginary dove
> That inflames the last loves,
> Soul of light, music, and flowers,
> Wandering imaginary dove.

11. Meredith, *Modern Love,* Sonnet 47.

12. James Joyce, *Finnegans Wake* (Harmondsworth: Penguin, 1976; rpt. 1999), 216 (end of Book 1). The whole passage runs: "Who were Shem and Shaun the living sons or daughters of? Night now! Tell me, tell me, tell me, elm! Night night! Telmetale of stem or stone. Beside the rivering waters of, hitherandthithering waters of. Night!" Borges' attitude toward Joyce's last novel is ambiguous: "The justification for the whole period lies in the two works by Joyce, . . . of which *Finnegans Wake,* whose protagonist is the English language, is ineluctably unreadable, and certainly untranslatable into Spanish." See Roberto Alifano, *Conversaciones con Borges* (Madrid: Debate, 1986), 115.

13. These lines from "Report on Experience," by Edmund Blunden (1896–1974), gain power from the fact that they echo, in inverted form, a passage from the King James

version of the Bible: "I have been young, and now am old; yet have I not seen the righteous forsaken, nor his seed begging bread" (Psalms 37:25).

14. "Luck! In the house of breathings lies that word, all fairness. The walls are of rubinen and the glittergates of elfinbone. The roof herof is of massicious jasper and a canopy of Tyrian awning rises and still descends to it." James Joyce, *Finnegans Wake,* 249 (Book 2).

15. Samuel Johnson's *Dictionary of the English Language* was published in London in 1755. Walter W. Skeat's *Etymological Dictionary of the English Language* was first published in Oxford, England, 1879–1882. *The Shorter Oxford English Dictionary* (based on the twelve-volume *OED*) was first published in Oxford in 1933.

16. Robert Louis Stevenson, *Memories and Portraits* (1887), Chapter 4: "I have thus played the sedulous ape to Hazlitt, to Lamb, to Wordsworth, to Sir Thomas Browne, to Defoe, to Hawthorne, to Montaigne, to Baudelaire, and to Obermann."

17. Samuel Taylor Coleridge, *Biographia Literaria,* Chapter 14: "that willing suspension of disbelief for the moment, which constitutes poetic faith."

18. These are the last four lines of Samuel Taylor Coleridge's "Kubla Khan."

19. Azorín (1873–1967), *La ruta de Don Quijote* (Buenos Aires: Losada, 1974). Miguel de Unamuno (1864–1936), *Vida de Don Quijote y Sancho según Miguel de Cervantes Saavedra,* 2nd ed. (Madrid: Renacimiento, 1913).

20. "To draw the longbow" means "to tell tall tales," "to make exaggerated statements."

21. "A violent green peacock, deliriated/unlillied in gold."

22. *Paradise Regained,* Book 4, lines 638–639; in *The Complete Works of John Milton,* ed. John T. Shawcross (New York: Doubleday, 1990), 572.

23. From Milton's sonnet on his blindness, "When I Consider How My Light Is Spent" (1673).

6. A Poet's Creed

1. John Keats, "Ode to a Nightingale," lines 61–67 (stanza 7).

2. Borges had dealt extensively with this issue in "Los traductores de las *1001 noches*" (The Translators of the Thousand and One Nights), included in his 1936 volume *La historia de la eternidad.* The scholar Antoine Galland (1646–1715) published his French translation of the *Thousand and One Nights* in the years 1704–1717. The British orientalist Edward William Lane (1801–1876) published his English translation in 1838–1840.

3. The phrase is from Whitman's *Leaves of Grass* (1892 edition), "Song of Myself," section 24, line 1.

4. "El inmortal" (The Immortal) was first published in 1949, in Borges' collection *El Aleph.*

5. Virgil, *Aeneid,* Book 6, line 268. In John Dryden's translation the line runs: "Obscure they went thro' dreary shades" (Book 6, line 378). Robert D. Williams renders it

as: "They walked exploring the unpeopled night" (Book 6, line 355).

6. From *The Seafarer,* ed. Ida Gordon (Manchester, England: Manchester University Press, 1979), 37. See Borges' discussion in Chapter 1 of this volume.

7. Shakespeare, Sonnet 8.

8. This is the first line of Keats's "Endymion" (1818).

9. Borges, in conversation with Willis Barnstone, expressed a desire for anonymity. "'If the Bible is peacock feathers, what kind of bird are you?' I asked. 'I am,' Borges answered, 'the bird's *egg,* in its Buenos Aires nest, unhatched, gladly unseen by anyone with discrimination, and I emphatically hope it will stay that way!'" Willis Barnstone, *With Borges on an Ordinary Evening in Buenos Aires: A Memoir* (Urbana: University of Illinois Press, 1993), 2.

10. "Spinoza" was published in a volume dedicated to Leopoldo Lugones, *El otro, el mismo* (The Self and the Other) (Buenos Aires: Emecé Editores, 1966). The translation runs thus:

> The Jew's hands, translucent in the dusk,
> Polish the lenses time and again.
> The dying afternoon is fear, is
> Cold, and all afternoons are the same.
> The hands and the hyacinth-blue air
> That whitens at the ghetto edges
> Do not quite exist for this silent
> Man who conjures up a clear labyrinth,
> Undisturbed by fame—that reflection

> Of dreams in the dream of another
> Mirror—or by maidens' timid love.
> Free of metaphor and myth, he grinds
> A stubborn crystal: the infinite
> Map of the One who is all His stars.

Translated by Richard Howard and César Rennert, in Jorge Luis Borges, *Selected Poems, 1923–1967,* ed. Norman Thomas di Giovanni (New York: Delacorte Press, 1972), 193. A second sonnet devoted to the philosopher, "Baruch Spinoza," was published in *La moneda de hierro* (The Iron Coin) in 1976, and translated by Willis Barnstone:

> A haze of gold, the Occident lights up
> The window. Now, the assiduous manuscript
> Is waiting, weighed down with the infinite.
> Someone is building God in a dark cup.
> A man engenders God. He is a Jew
> With saddened eyes and lemon-colored skin;
> Time carries him the way a leaf, dropped in
> A river, is borne off by waters to
> Its end. No matter. The magician moved
> Carves out his God with fine geometry;
> From his disease, from nothing, he's begun
> To construct God, using the word. No one
> Is granted such prodigious love as he:
> The love that has no hope of being loved.

Barnstone, *With Borges on an Ordinary Evening in Buenos Aires,* 5. For the original, see Borges, *Obras completas,* vol. 3 (Buenos Aires: Emecé Editores, 1995), 151.

OF THIS AND THAT

VERSATILE CRAFT

Calin-Andrei Mihailescu

When Borges came to Harvard in the fall of 1967 to deliver the Norton Lectures, he had long been deemed precious capital. In his self-deprecating way, he claimed to be something of an Invisible Man in his own country, yet his North American contemporaries seemed certain (polite enthusiasm apart) that his was one of the names destined to survive through time's long run. We know that thus far they were not mistaken: Borges has resisted the usual effacement of

I would like to thank Melitta Adamson, Sherri Clendinning, Richard Green, Christina Johnson, Gloria Koyounian, Thomas Orange, Andrew Szeib, Jane Toswell, and Marek Urban. Without their help, my efforts to get these lectures into book form would have been more painful. I am most indebted to Maria Ascher, senior editor at Harvard University Press, whose professionalism and utter devotion to Borges made this book possible.

time,* and the charm and power of this forget-
ting-dodger's work are undiminished. For more than
thirty years the six lectures never made it into print,
the tapes gathering dust in the quiet ever-after of a library vault. When they had gathered enough, they
were found. The spectacular precedent of Igor Stravinsky's *Poetics of Music in the Form of Six Lessons,*
delivered as Norton Lectures in 1939–1940 and published by Harvard University Press in 1970, shows
that a long delay in the transition to print need not de-
prive lectures of their relevance. Borges' have as
much appeal now as they had three decades ago.

This Craft of Verse is an introduction to literature,
to taste, and to Borges himself. In the context of his
complete works, it compares only with *Borges, oral*
(1979), which contains the five lectures—somewhat
narrower in scope than these—that he gave May–June
1978 at the University of Belgrano in Buenos Aires.†

---

* With his customary irony, Borges declared that he was not as
good at mocking himself as other writers—his great friend Adolfo
Bioy Casares among them. "It consoles me to know that I will be dis-
solved by forgetfulness. Forgetting will make me anonymous, will it
not?" *Borges—Bioy: Confesiones, confesiones*, ed. Rodolfo Braceli
(Buenos Aires: Sudamericana, 1997), 51–52.

† *Borges, oral* contains the "personal part" of those Belgrano lectures. The topics include (in chronological order) the book, immor-

These Norton Lectures, which precede *Borges, oral* by a decade, are a treasury of literary riches that come to us in essayistic, unassuming, often ironic, and always stimulating forms.

The first lecture, "The Riddle of Poetry," delivered on October 24, 1967, deals with the ontological status of poetry and effectively leads us into the volume as a whole. "The Metaphor" (delivered November 16) discusses, on the model of Leopoldo Lugones, the way in which poets through the centuries have used and reused the same metaphorical patterns, which, Borges suggests, can be reduced to twelve "essential affinities," the rest being merely designed to astonish and therefore ephemeral. In "The Telling of the Tale" (December 6), devoted to epic poetry, Borges comments on the modern world's neglect of the epic, speculates about the death of the novel, and looks at the way the contemporary human condition is reflected in the ideology of the novel: "We do not really believe in happi-

---

tality, Swedenborg, the detective story, and time. *Borges, oral* was first published by Emecé Editores in Buenos Aires in 1979, and was reprinted in Borges, *Obras completas*, vol. 4 (Buenos Aires: Emecé Editores, 1996), 161–205. Since its publication, it has become a standard reference for Borges scholars and for readers in the Hispanic world.

ness, and this is one of the poverties of our time." Here he shows affinities with Walter Benjamin and Franz Kafka (the latter of whom he considered a lesser writer than G. B. Shaw or G. K. Chesterton): he advocates the immediacy of storytelling and seems something of an anti-novelist, invoking laziness as the main reason for not having written novels. "Word-Music and Translation" (February 28, 1968) is a virtuoso meditation on the translation of poetry. "Thought and Poetry" (March 20) illustrates his essayistic rather than theoretical take on the status of literature. While holding that magical, musical truth is more potent than reason's stable fictions, Borges argues that meaning in poetry is a fetish, and that powerful metaphors unsettle hermeneutic frameworks rather than enhancing meaning. Finally, "A Poet's Creed" (April 10) is a confessional text, a kind of literary testament that he composed "in the middle of life's way." In 1968 Borges was still at the height of his powers and would yet publish first-rate works, such as *El informe de Brodie* (Dr. Brodie's Report; 1970)—which contains "La Intrusa" (The Intruder), the story he claimed was his best—and *El libro de arena* (The Book of Sand; 1975).

These Norton Lectures were delivered by a seer who has often been ranked with the other "great blind men of the West." Borges' unfailing admiration for Homer, his high but complex praise for Joyce, and his thinly disguised doubt of Milton say much about this tradition. His progressive blindness had become nearly total by the 1960s, when he was able to see nothing more than an amorphous field of yellow. He dedicated *El oro de los tigres* (The Gold of the Tigers; 1972) to this last and most loyal color of his world. Borges' style of delivery was as singular as it was compelling: while speaking, he would look upward with a gentle and shy expression on his face, seeming to materially touch the world of the texts—their colors, fabric, music. Literature, for him, was a mode of experience.

Unlike the brusque and idiosyncratic tone that characterizes most of his Spanish interviews and public lectures, Borges' manner in *This Craft of Verse* is that of a versatile and soft-spoken guest of honor. Yet this book, though wonderfully accessible, does not offer easy-to-munch-on teachings; rather, it is full of deeply personal reflections, and is neither naive nor cynical. It preserves the immediacy of its oral delivery—its flow, humor, and occasional hesitations. (Borges' syntax has been altered here only as much as is necessary to make the prose grammatical and readable. Also, occasional misquotations on his part have been corrected.) This spoken-written text addresses its audience with informality and much warmth.

Borges' facility with English is charming. He learned the language in his early childhood from his paternal grandmother, who had come to Buenos Aires from Staffordshire. Both his parents knew English well (his father was a professor of psychology and modern languages; his mother, a translator). Borges spoke it fluidly, musically, with delicate consonants, and took particular delight in the "stark and voweled" sound of Old English.

One cannot quite take at face value Borges' claim that he is "groping" his way along, that he is a "timid thinker rather than a daring one," and that his cultural background is "a series of unfortunate miscellanies."* Borges was immensely learned, and one of the chief themes of his work—the theme of the world as an infinite library—has clear autobiographical connotations. His memory was extraordinary: he delivered these six lectures without the help of notes, since his poor eyesight made it impossible for him to read.†

* See Chapter 2; also *Borges—Bioy: Confesiones, confesiones*, III.

† Borges' memory was legendary. An American professor of Romanian origin reports that, during a chat with Borges in 1976 at the University of Indiana, the Argentine writer recited to him an

Aided by this remarkable mnemonic capacity, Borges enriches his lectures with myriad textual examples—his aesthetics is always rooted in the primary ground of literature. For literary theorists, he does not have much use; for critics, he has just a little; and philosophers interest him only to the extent that their ideas do not forsake the world for pure abstraction. Thus, his remembering of world literature lives the *belles lettres* as he speaks.

In *This Craft of Verse,* Borges converses with authors and texts he never lost the pleasure of requoting and discussing, sources ranging from Homer, Virgil, *Beowulf,* the Norse Eddas, the *Thousand and One Nights,* the Koran, and the Bible, to Rabelais, Cervantes, Shakespeare, Keats, Heine, Poe, Stevenson, Whitman, Joyce, and of course himself.

Borges' greatness is due in part to a wit and polish that characterize not only his works but his life as well. Asked whether he had ever been visited in his dreams by Juan Perón (the Argentine dictator, and

---

eight-stanza Romanian poem which he had learned from its author, a young refugee, in Geneva in 1916. Borges did not know Romanian. The power of his memory was also peculiar in that he tended to remember words and works by others, while claiming to have completely forgotten texts that he himself had written.

widower of Evita), Borges retorted: "My dreams have their style—there is no way I will have him in my dreams."*

* *Borges—Bioy: Confesiones, confesiones*, 60. Other collections of interviews with Borges include *Dos palabras antes de morir y otras entrevistas*, ed. Fernando Mateo (Buenos Aires: LC Editor, 1994); *Borges, el memorioso: Conversaciones de Jorge Luis Borges con Antonio Carrizo* (Mexico City: Fondo de Cultura Económica, 1982); *Borges: Imágenes, memorias, diálogos*, ed. María Esther Vázquez, 2nd ed. (Caracas: Monte Ávila, 1980); and Jorge Luis Borges and Osvaldo Ferrari, *Diálogos últimos* (Buenos Aires: Sudamericana, 1987).

INDEX

Alfred, King, 52, 79
America, 3, 53
Anglo-Saxon. *See* Old English
Arabian Nights, 36, 46, 51, 67, 82, 98, 101–102, 149
Ariosto, Ludovico: *Orlando Furioso*, 51
Arnold, Matthew, 66–68
Augustine, Saint, 19
Azorín: *La ruta de Don Quijote*, 93

Barbusse, Henri: *Le Feu*, 52
"Battle of Brunanburh," 38, 58–59, 62–64
Baudelaire, Charles, 107; *Les Fleurs du mal*, 74
Benjamin, Walter, 146
Beowulf, 11, 22–23, 51, 149
Berkeley, George, 2–3, 83
Bible, 7, 9–10, 25, 46–48, 67–68, 72–73, 82, 149
Blunden, Edmund, 89
Borges, oral, 144–145
Browne, Thomas, 111

Browning, Elizabeth Barrett: *Sonnets from the Portuguese*, 73
Browning, Robert, 14–15
Buber, Martin, 31–32
Buddha, 7
Buenos Aires, 5, 32, 98, 148
Bunyan, John: *The Pilgrim's Progress*, 109
Burton, Richard, 67, 98, 101
Butler, Samuel, 45
Byron, George Gordon, Lord: "She Walks in Beauty," 39–40

Calderón de la Barca, Pedro, 69
Campbell, Roy, 61, 64–65
Cansinos-Asséns, Rafael, 8, 15
Carlyle, Thomas: *Sartor Resartus*, 104–105, 110
Cervantes, Miguel de, 149; *Don Quixote*, 11–12, 93, 102–103, 108
Chapman, George, 4–6, 76
Chaucer, Geoffrey, 48, 62

Chesterton, G. K., 17, 81, 146;
    "The Ballad of the White
    Horse," 52–54; "A Second
    Childhood," 24
China, 2, 21, 33
Christianity, 8
Chuan Tzu, 29–30
Coleridge, Samuel Taylor, 92
Conrad, Joseph, 48
Crane, Stephen: *The Red Badge of
    Courage*, 100
Croce, Benedetto, 2, 117
Cummings, E. E., 33–34

Dante Alighieri, 54; *Divine Com-
    edy*, 3
Darío, Rubén, 50, 86
De Quincey, Thomas, 2, 93
Dickens, Charles, 12
Donne, John, 95
Dostoevsky, Feodor, 104
Doyle, Arthur Conan: *Adventures
    of Sherlock Holmes*, 94, 103,
    108
Dujovne, León, 32

Elizabeth, Queen, 84
Emerson, Ralph Waldo, 3, 31, 106
England, 17, 64, 80
English language, 10–11, 13, 67–68,
    85, 101, 148

Farid al-Din Attar, 35; *Parliament
    of Birds*, 69
Fernández, Macedonio, 8
Finnesburg, fragment of, 32
FitzGerald, Edward, 69–71
Flaubert, Gustave: *Salammbô*, 112
Freire, Ricardo Jaimes, 86

French language, 11, 40, 118
Frost, Robert: "Acquainted with
    the Night," 108; "Stopping by
    Woods on a Snowy Evening,"
    30–31, 107–108

Galland, Antoine, 101
Geneva, 104
George, Stefan: *Blumen des Böse*,
    74
German language, 68, 74, 104–105
Gibbon, Edward, 116
Gnosticism, 109
Goethe, Johann Wolfgang von:
    Wilhelm Meisters Lehrjahre, 111
Góngora y Argote, Luis de, 38–39,
    95
Gospels, 7, 46–48
Greece, 2, 7–8, 13–14, 24–26, 45,
    88
Greek Anthology, 24

Hafiz of Shiraz, 35
Hanslick, Eduard, 77, 87
Harvard University, 143
Hawthorne, Nathaniel: *The Scar-
    let Letter*, 77
Hazlitt, William, 92
Hebrews, 10, 68, 82
Heine, Heinrich, 30, 149; *Lyrisches
    Intermezzo*, 104
Hengist of Ephesus, 64, 80
Heraclitus, 26
Hölderlin, Friedrich, 105
Holy Ghost, 9–10, 15, 72
Homer, 3–4, 10, 13–14, 16, 18, 30,
    55, 66, 72, 75–76, 147, 149; *Iliad*,
    5–6, 32, 44–45, 71, 113; *Odyssey*,
    5–6, 45–46, 71, 76

INDEX

Horsa, 64
Hume, David, 2

India, 2, 75, 114
Islam, 9

James, Henry, 118; *The Aspern Papers*, 49
Jáuregui, Juan de, 71
Jesus, 7, 47, 99
Jews, 10, 68, 82
John, Saint, 25
John of the Cross, Saint, 60–62, 64
Johnson, Samuel, 91
Joyce, James, 95, 147, 149; *Finnegans Wake*, 88–90; *Ulysses*, 54
Judas, 99–100

Kabbalah, 72, 82
Kafka, Franz, 146; *The Castle*, 49–50
Keats, John, 115, 149; "Ode to a Nightingale," 98–100; "On First Looking into Chapman's Homer," 4–6
Khayyám, Omar: *Rubáiyát*, 35, 69–71
Kipling, Rudyard, 106, 118; *From Sea to Sea*, 36; "A Sahib's War," 52
Koran, 9, 149

Lane, Edward William, 101
Lang, Andrew, 25, 44
Langland, William, 46
Latin, 111, 115

Lawrence, T. E.: *Seven Pillars of Wisdom*, 52
León, Fray Luis de, 3, 68
Lessing, Gotthold, 105
London, 4
Longfellow, Henry Wadsworth, 26
Lucan, 71
Lugones, Leopoldo, 86, 94, 106, 145; *Lunario sentimental*, 22
Luther, Martin, 68

Manrique, Jorge, 26
Melville, Herman, 48; *Moby-Dick*, 108–109
Mencken, H. L., 49
Meredith, George, 83, 86–87
Milton, John, 10, 147; *Paradise Regained*, 47, 95
Morris, William, 85
Muslims, 9

Newman, Francis William, 66
Nibelungenlied, 105
Norton Lectures, 143–144

Old English, 9–11, 16–18, 22–23, 37–38, 58–59, 63–64, 80, 105, 115, 148–149
Old Norse, 9, 37–38, 73
Oxford Book of Modern Verse, The, 61

Paris, 6
Pater, Walter, 77
Perón, Juan, 149–150
Persian language, 35, 69–71, 73
Plato, 24; *Phaedrus*, 7–8
Poe, Edgar Allan, 50, 106–107, 149
Pope, Alexander, 66, 71, 76, 113

Prescott, William: *History of the Conquest of Peru*, 98
Psycho (film), 50
Pythagoras, 7

Rabelais, François, 76, 149
Revelation, Book of, 25
Rome, 116
Rossetti, Dante Gabriel, 12–13, 18, 69
Rouse, W. H. D., 44

Sandburg, Carl, 110
Scholasticism, 2
Schopenhauer, Arthur, 2, 8, 83, 105
Scots, 81
Scott, Walter: *Ivanhoe*, 112
Seneca, 8
Shakespeare, William, 5, 28, 35, 37, 46, 54, 84–85, 149; *Hamlet*, 11; *Macbeth*, 3
Shaw, Bernard, 7, 9, 149
Shorter Oxford English Dictionary, 91
Skeat, Walter W., 22, 91
Socrates, 7–8
"Song of Songs," 65, 68
Spanish language, 60, 70–71, 85, 111, 121, 147
Spengler, Oswald: *The Decline of the West*, 9
Spinoza, Baruch, 83, 121
Stevenson, Robert Louis, 78, 80, 89, 91–92, 106, 110, 149; *Dr. Jekyll and Mr. Hyde*, 50; "Requiem," 90–91; *Weir of Hermiston*, 27

Stravinsky, Igor: *Poetics of Music in the Form of Six Lessons*, 144
Sturluson, Snorri, 45
Swinburne, Algernon Charles, 69
Symons, Arthur, 61

Tacitus, 105
Tennyson, Alfred, 25, 58–59, 62–64
Twain, Mark: *Adventures of Huckleberry Finn*, 102; *Life on the Mississippi*, 102; *Roughing It*, 102

Unamuno, Miguel de: *Vida de Don Quijote y Sancho*, 93
University of Belgrano, 144
Urquhart, Thomas, 76

Verlaine, Paul, 114
Virgil, 45, 55, 115, 149
Vogelweide, Walther von der, 28–29, 35
Völsunga Saga, 51

Watts, G. F., 81
Wells, H. G.: *The Invisible Man*, 120
Whistler, James McNeill, 6
Whitehead, Alfred North, 80
Whitman, Walt, 32, 110, 149; *Leaves of Grass*, 104
Wilde, Oscar, 106
Wolfe, Thomas: *Of Time and the River*, 26
Wordsworth, William, 43, 114

Yeats, William Butler, 61, 82–83, 95; "Leda and the Swan," 78

INDEX